THE BEST OF THE FIRST

The Early Days
Of Rock and Roll

by
Bob Kinder

ADAMS PRESS
CHICAGO, ILLINOIS

LIBRARY OF CONGRESS
CATALOG CARD NUMBER 86-90780

ISBN 0-9616805-0-4

PRINTED IN THE
UNITED STATES OF AMERICA

This book is dedicated to the memory of my late father, Harold Robert Kinder, who knew how to live in harmony and rhythm with his fellow man. I also dedicate my book to my wonderful mother who inspired me and to my sister, Lila May Gallant Armshaw and to my little nephew—Jamie!

I hope in future generations that music and the ability to entertain and enjoy ourselves will always be with us.

Harold Robert Kinder—Savannah, Missouri (1973)

iii

ACKNOWLEDGMENTS

I would like to thank the following relatives, friends and contributors who helped make this work possible—my parents, Harold and Margery Kinder, Lila May Gallant Armshaw, Marvin and Lois Kinder, Ruth G., Irene, Don Kinder, and the late Jake Montgomery who worked at my Uncle Don's Cosmopolitan Shoe (repair-shine) Shop and in the past, told me inspiring stories of the St. Joseph honky tonk scene near the river front in the forties and fifties when the late Coleman "Bean" Hawkins and the late great Joe Turner played their jiving rhythms in the colored back houses along the Missouri River bottoms in and around the downtown red light district. I also want to additionally thank Tom Buetow, Tommy Keel, Lloyd Arnold, Club 45, Kay Martin, Martin Affleck, Gene Vincent, Jerry Lee Lewis, Carl Perkins, Joyce, Wayne Cochran, Floyd Williams, Chuck Jackson, Jerry Muse, Dan Evans, Jim McCrary, Gorgeous George, Little Willie John, Wanda Jackson, Sam Davidson, Dale Brizendine, Jim Cates (Jim's picture sleeve guide is the greatest!!!), Billy Kretzer, Charlie Genova, Sherry, Joan, Joey Dee, Becky (for her patience), Jane Holbert, Kevin Garvis, Ray Childers, Kenny Brown (where are you now, Kenny?), Colby Atwood (keep on keepin' on singing your songs, Colby!), Bill Swopes, Chris Fritz, Whit Pell, Don Hardman, Carrol Howard, Rick Whitesell (for inspiration), Peter A. Grendysa (for writing inspirational articles and keeping alive and in print feature stories on early rock and roll singers), Dennis Klopp, Baron Yama, Karen Wheeler, Cotton (for being so creative in making his first guitar from a tree), and the New York rock and roll promoters including Dick Fox, Tony DeLauro, and Richard Nader for keeping early rock alive with their great Big Apple concerts.

The majority of the pictures published in this volume were originally photographed by the author including the shots of Jerry Lee Lewis, Gene Vincent, Carl Perkins, Gorgeous George, Diana Ross, Conway Twitty, Chuck Berry, Little Richard, etc., and the many other pics used in this volume are from the author's own private collection (and sources unknown). I want to also thank Rosemary Fullmer Spoonamore for the Freddie Cannon pics, and Columbia, Capitol, A&M, Smash-Mercury, RCA, and Atlantic Records.

TABLE OF CONTENTS

FOREWORD

Rock and roll music will make us laugh;
and it will even make us cry;
but I don't care 'cause
I'll be rockin'
'till the day I die—(Bob Kinder)

A 1950's WHB rock and roll dee jay—Kansas City, Missouri (note the records)

ROCK RADIO

In 1952, Cleveland's WTW DJ, Alan Freed, coined the term "Rock and Roll" from a bluesy type music that was wooing white teenagers at a local record shop owned by proprietor Leo Mintz. Songs by Wynonnie Harris, The Orioles, The Clovers, Piano Red, and Louis Jordan were making white teenagers rock as well as roll. This so-called "Race" music was becoming mainstream pop by 1955 thanks to Freed's airplay exposure on WINS New York along with his rock and roll spectaculars at the Brooklyn Paramount and Brooklyn Fox Theatres.

On any given night, a rock and roll buff may see on stage the pick of the litter performing their recordings live. The Moonglows would warble some of their chess classics "See Saw" or "We Belong Together" while Gene Vincent and his riotous Blue Caps would turn the theatre upside down with "Race With The Devil." Jo Ann Campbell was the favorite for the male patrons with her busty blond features that included hip-hugger dark colored slacks and tight fitting knit sweaters A la Dolly Parton. Her raspy vocalized version of Elvis Presley's "Hound Dog" would bring all the macho men to their knees while balladeer Teddy Randazzo won out with the ladies.

Elvis was its undisputed king while Alan Freed was the father of rock and roll and pioneered the rock and roll shows in Cleveland. There were occasions when Freed shared the King tag with Presley especially during promotional hype for Freed's movies like "Rock, Rock, Rock," and "Mister Rock and Roll," during 1957-'58.

Alan Freed's downfall was threefold. First, he refused to play white covers of black recordings by steadfastly playing the originals. Secondly, Freed was the scapegoat for the Payola Scandal that shook the radio-recording industry in the late fifties. Today, when asked if Payola still exists all those that were interviewed by a 1985 cable network investigation into the practice inside the industry responded with a "No Comment." Thirdly, Freed admitted to some of the charges but in spite of his honesty, they literally buried him. For example, after a Boston rock and roll show that Freed promoted in 1958 that headlined Jerry Lee Lewis, Freed left town with no rioting and little disturbance the night of the concert. But the city brought Freed back for a court date in which they slapped an indictment against Freed for inciting a riot and attempting to overthrow the government. For the latter charge, the Boston officials pulled out of the hat an anarchy law from the 19th century intermingled between other laws which forbade citizens from leaving their horses unattended.

A state senator charged also that Freed's audiences were using drugs but the charge was unproven. The FBI even stepped in and investigated Freed's acts followed by the IRS and this witch hunt soon relegated Freed to becoming a typical run of the mill DJ in Los Angeles and later Florida. Freed died in 1965 after working on a blues and jazz station that featured recordings by such artists as B. B. King and jazz organist, Jimmy Smith.

George Tucker was a New York personality, who like Freed, exploited the commercialism of rock and roll. Tucker tagged himself as the "King of the Golden Oldies" and produced one of the finest oldies compilations ever put together in 1962 with "Twenty Original Golden Oldies" for the Mr. Maestro label out of New York.

Another pioneer in rock and roll radio was George "Hound Dog" Lorenz in Buffalo, New York. The Hound Dog made such an everlasting impression on his fans that Atlantic Records dedicated an album titled "Hound Dog's Solid Gold," a compilation of Lorenz's favorite faves.

Dick Clark in 1958 during the Washington investigation had similar problems as Freed's and was accused of conflicts of interest in hosting his Philadelphia-based TV'er, "American Bandstand" and financial investments in Swan Records and other artists affiliated with other companies such as Duane Eddy of Jamie Records. Clark at the time was also accused of being "The Czar of the Switchblade Set" by supporting and promoting teenage entertainment.

Dick Clark eventually just received a slap on the wrist while Alan Freed was massacred over The Payola Scandal that can be likened to Custer's last stand at Little Big Horn.

A former member of Bill Haley's Comets twelve years later, confided to this writer that Dick Clark actually was offering such bids of at least five thousand dollars for Haley's right to appear on Bandstand.

While the late Murray "The K" Kaufman became the top New York DJ host of rock and roll spectaculars at the Brooklyn Fox, Philadelphia's Jerry Blavat, known affectionately as "The Geator With The Heator" kept personality radio happening alongside the music in the early to mid-sixties.

Blavat was a long time Little Richard fan and was among the first to feature Richard, who returned to rock after becoming a preacher, during an hour long session on his nationally syndicated mid-sixties TV Show.

Top forty radio was ultimately the brainchild of Ted Storz who revamped the musical mode of presentation on his stations KOWH in Omaha and WHB in Kansas City.

Gordon McClendon who was a self-made millionaire and an astute entrepreneur out of the fifties helped start top forty radio in Dallas, San Antonio, Houston as well as star in B-Movie exploitation horror flicks over thirty years ago. McClendon has to be credited for his foresight in dipping into the top forty venture early in the game.

Top forty formatted radio was simply a system whereby slick hip talking jocks cracked jokes over the air while playing mostly fast-paced recordings by Elvis, Buddy Holly and others, while at the same time using catchy lyrical melodies to station identification jingles and on the hour newsbreak that would last only a few minutes in actual length.

Today, radio is governed and controlled by corporation magnates, record company consultants who call on stations to get their artists aired, and program directors who use planned spots by rotation whereby a slow song usually follows a fast one. The songs played usually follows what is currently popular on the Billboard charts.

Today, the stations which were formally top forty in nature now has honed themselves into a top five listing whereby the most popular songs at any given time is rotated back and forth being played two to four times per hour to assure that station's highest listenership. The fight for the top advertising dollars on the market today is highly competitive and so intense that it is on a level with mediocrity whereby very few new break-in artists get any kind of proper attention in order to be added to the play lists with MTV and VHI. The cornerstone of today's creativity is being expanded somewhat but variety still seems to be a thing of the past.

In spite of a gloomy musical picture in the last decade, there still seems to be hope for the future artists like Sade and The Manhatten Transfer who are keeping popular music alive and lively.

"Cousin" Bruce Morrow, a music program show host on the Eastern Seaboard for over twenty-five years, was interviewed on a popular nation-wide cable program and hinted that the "personality" disc jockeys are on their way back to popularity once again in 1985.

Not too many years ago, the so-called "personality" jocks had devout followers by their trendy on and off-color jokes and straight from the hip jive talk that set these delightful crazies apart from the bland run of the mill day or night hosts. These madmen of the audio era of popular music were as important, if not in some cases more so, as the music they were featuring on the airwaves. For example, Pogo Poge, a Maynard G. Krebs look alike from the late fifties was a Beatnik imaged DJ flipping his lid on KIMN Radio in Denver during the early sixties while "Rockin'" Bob Robbin on WHB in Kansas City was churning the hits including his rockin' with Robbin theme, Bobby Day's class 1958 recording, "Rockin' Robbin." Some of the other more colorful disk jockeys also included Dick Biondi on Chicago's power-house channel, WLS, Robin Seymour on WKMH in Detroit, Philadelphia's Joe Niagra on WIBG, and Arnie "Woo Woo" Ginsburg was strong on Boston's WMEX in the early sixties while the late Jack Carney was wooing his listeners in St. Louis on WIL radio in the late fifties and sixties. Many of the aforementioned with the exception of Pogo Poge and Bob Robbin were a part of the "Cruisin" series of albums on the Increase label that was featuring the aforementioned personalities on the fifties and sixties series of albums detailing the history of Rock and Roll Radio.

John R. Richardson, the famed all night rhythm and blues radio show host in Nashville during the early sixties, etched out notoriety with his bassy nasal gravely voice box that was a distinct trademark for him as he continuously was spinning deep soul selections. Although

5

his playlist recordings didn't always make the Billboard charts, they nonetheless rated highly with his listeners.

Richardson would often feature "once in a lifetime" record deals that would come from Ernie's Record Shop. John R's successful brand of quick talkin' jive was reflective in his ear-catching advertisements in which he would sell anything and everything that would come through mail order like baby chicks to offering a chance for his insomniac listeners to invest their few precious dollars into a live mink ranch. "John R here darlin' and I have a special announcement for ya—"

In 1955, Dewey Phillips was the first DJ to play Elvis records on his "Red Hot and Blue" WHBQ Radio show in Memphis.

The top rockin' rollin' daddy in radio during 1959 ironically wasn't found in the states but in Mexico instead. The soulful Dr. Jazzmo was the "Boss with the Red Hot Sauce" on XERF across the Del Rio, Texas border into Mexico. His exuberant flashy radio mannerisms and raw down to earth delivery were so effective that his enthusiasm would believably light up an evergreen at Christmas time. He would scat hip slang in between playing a B. B. King or a Roscoe Gordon disk and would feature record discount packages such as "The 1959 B. B. King Record Special—You can get six records baby for only $5.98 postpaid." Jazzmo would launch into King's "Sweet Sixteen" and effectively come back into another commercial break by hyping a commercially sponsored product—"Baby, now you can git if ya' orda' raight naw a once in a lifetime offa a big juicy gitar fa' only ten dolla' babyee—just think you can learn how to play the gitar like B. B. King that comes with an instruction booklet for only ten dolla."

By 1961, Doctor Jazzmo was replaced by a heaving growling madman who billed himself Wolfman Jack. His insanity included lecturing and talking to his wolf friend, "Marrio" who would supposedly howl through the predominately blues records he featured from 12:00-5:00 A.M.

The Wolfman would butcher records on the air by singing along during different intervals on such "A" sides as James Brown's "Papa's Got A Brand New Bag" or Arthur Conley's "Who Fooling Who."

Wolfman Jack would get everybody to party with him with such convincing tongue lashings as "We're gonna' get down in the alley with this one by Lowell Fulson Children—we're gonna get down in the alley, baby!"

"This next song is gonna turn your toenail up baby—it's gonna turn your toenail up now."

"I'm gonna git my little brown bottle baby and I'm gonna' hit the floor like grandpa and boogie chillen all over the place."

If these aforementioned statements didn't crack rib cages then Wolfman would mention the stations call letters XERF often followed by reminding his North of the border fans that "We're down South with the donkey, baby." He will also invite his followers to "Get yourself naked."

Wolfman in 1963 recorded an album of classic rock selections with the (New Orleans) Rhythm Kings in Oklahoma City, whereby he parodied hits like "Short Fat Fannie" and "New Orleans." The Wolfman would advertise the album over the air and remind everyone that "You gonna love this record to death baby—you outta git it in your home so you can drive all your neighbors crazy—aw—right!!"

Like so many of his forerunners, the Wolfman would peddle items that would make strange bedfellows in any home environment such as the motion picture's still picture of Lon Chaney's horrific movie creature, the original Wolfman advertised and sold on the impression of boing an actual self portrait of the one and only Wolfman Jack to florescent pictures of Jesus the would actually glow in the dark.

In his early days, the Wolfman's true picture and identity remained a closely guarded secret. He would not identify himself to anyone. This well kept secret was later depicted in George Lucas' film, "American Graffiti." Wolfman, of course, later came out of his underground closet on his 500,000 watted pirate station in Mexico to become a nationally syndicated radio celebrity whose yearly earnings would only be topped by New York City's Don Imus.

The Wolfman, whose real name is Bob Smith, also became a popular music host on NBC's "Midnight Special." As his commercial popularity grew, the Wolfman found himself prostituted like Dick Clark as he also had to stay in sync with his fame by playing the top commercial hits of the day a la Stones, Beatles, etc. and thereby leave his dearly beloved rhythm and blues and soul obscurities behind him.

What is his great goal and yearning?

"Someday," he candidly explained to this interviewer, "When all this madness (commercial success) is over with, I want to go back behind the border and slip away and play my blues (records) again."

GENE VINCENT — 1959

In January, 1959, a major rock and roll production unfolded at Saint Joseph, Missouri's Municipal Auditorium. The event was a very historic one indeed, except for the fact that very few people in this historic Northwest community realized just how big a concert this actually was.

The first group that appeared on stage were the Twisters from Texas. The group came dressed in all-red jump suits with a white-bearded sax player that put out some raspy hot sounds that enthralled the audience and got their fans clapping, and shaking in their seats. The Twisters were the same band that backed fellow Texan, Rod Bernard on his Arco recording, "This Should Go On Forever." This Texas-bred rocking hot foursome played some instrumental hits that cold January evening including Bill Doggett's "Honky Tonk" and the Viscount's big smash disc, "Harlem Nocturne." The Twister's lead saxophonist also performed some brilliant reed work on Johnny (Paris) and the Hurricaneses original of "Crossfire." This Texas outfit's crazy antics included jumping, leaping, running, falling and rolling all over the floor of the big stage while the small throng of about fifty concert customers showed their appreciation by dancing and clapping to the Twister's musical rhythms.

The Twisters remained on stage to back up the stellar rockabilly attractions that were scheduled to appear on this particular night's playbill. One of the rockers on the show was a young new artist from Kentucky by the name of Pat Kelly. Pat was introduced by the emcee as a new and upcoming rock and roll star. This southern rockabilly was all dressed out in western style garb with a spangled jacket and matching jeweled

9

trousers that would make even Roy Rogers and Gene Autry stand up and take notice. This promising premier vocalist was actually on his very first national debut tour in promoting his first recording on the Jubilee label titled "Hey Doll Baby." Pat sang in a rocking Elvis Presley—growling style. Pat Kelly and the Twisters kept up their non-stop grueling pace through several sizzling numbers for about twenty-five minutes before the set finally came to a dynamic close.

During a fifteen minute delay between acts in the show, the announcer notified the small but enthusiastic gathering that the evening's favorite attraction, Gene Vincent, was late in getting to the concert. It seems as though Gene's scheduled flight from California was delayed, due in part to foggy weather conditions. Gene was supposed to land at Saint Joseph's Rosecrans Airport.

When the second half of the show began, the Twisters opened up with some more dynamic tunes while the crowd was nervously waiting for the arrival of Mr. Be-Bop-A-Lula himself—Gene Vincent. By ten o'clock, it was announced that Gene and his small entourage had finally arrived via cab to the auditorium.

Gene Vincent came out from stage left dressed up in his street clothes which included powder-blue pants and a white dress shirt. It seems as though Gene didn't have time to come fully equipped in uniform and all his little extras, since he was late in arriving for the show.

Gene, that unforgettable night, proved to this midwestern community that Jesse James isn't the only rebel ever to invade this town. Gene proved that he is definitely one of the all-time greats in rock and roll. He even made my father's eyes shoot out of their sockets with his wild staged acrobatic gyrations that also included wrapping his entire body around the microphone stand. Gene rocked and stomped through close to one-half hour's worth of torrid rock and roll classics including "Whole Lotta Shakin' Goin' On," "Long Tall

Sally," and his all-time biggest seller for the capitol label in "Be-Bop-A-Lula." During the latter selection, Gene demonstrated a lot of finesse and enthusiasm by doing some hair-raising showmanship by hopping over the microphone. By the flash of an eyelash, Vincent twisted and tangled his entire body around the microphone and fell to the floor as if he was in agonized pain. Gene tormented and teased the crowd with some more acrobatic-styled choreographic vibrations by contorting and twisting his face and whole body around the microphone some more as his dark but tangled long hair came crashing down over his forehead into his eyes. The crowd yelled their enthusiasm and Gene came off the stage as the announcer came strolling out to the center of the floor to announce that GAC (General Artists Corporation) Attractions was about to set another booking for March in this venue that would star Frankie Avalon. Frankie Avalon at this time was having a big hit record on the charts with "Venus." Since there was such a small crowd for this evening's show, there were no more shows that were scheduled in this venue for a long time to come. (As an anecdote to this, it is indeed ironic that the next time any musical presentations were held in this Saint Joseph arena were booked by Harry "Hap" Pebbles, a Kansas City country music booking agent who later brought such luminaries to this city as Johnny Cash, Gordon Terry, Carl Perkins, Bob Luman, and many others, which is actually the same type of musical form (rockabilly) that was being presented this chilly January evening in 1959 when many people got to see for the first and certainly the only time, the raw and natural talents of Gene Vincent.)

In November, 1959, Gene did actually come back to Saint Joseph for one more appearance before he finally did leave for many countless tours in Great Britain and the continent of Europe. Gene and the Blue Caps appeared at the Crystal Ballroom in the Hotel Robidoux for the regular Friday night radio station KUSN record hop. Gene's great outfit featured the flawless artistry of "Gallopin'" Cliff Gallop, "Duke" Duplisse on drums, and the tenor sax-background vocals of Johnny Vincent.

The Blue Caps opened the night's activities with some jump numbers including "The Girl Can't Help It" and "Bo Diddley." Gene Vincent eventually came out in a one-piece green-colored jump-suit with his initials, GV, inscribed on his upper left pocket of his outfit. Gene might have been crippled by a motorcycle accident in his Navy days during a leave of abscence. But he proved to this small but enthusiastic teenage gathering that he was agile and still had some classy movements in his showmanship as Gene had demonstrated earlier in the year from his previous Saint Joseph appearance. Gene's left leg was in a brace which was a painful reminder of his bike mishap. (Cliff Gallop on a show with Gary Stites in Saint Joseph a year later, told this writer that Gene's left leg gave him unbearable pain often and that one part of his injured leg was no bigger around than a silver dollar.)

Gene showed how much stage presence he still had in every ounce of his body when he performed his hit records of the day including "Lotta Lovin'" and Little Richard's monster recording of "Long Tall Sally."

During his performance at this KUSN record show, Gene and the boys invited local popular DJ personality, Bob Martin, to come up and play the drums and chant along with the Blue Caps on several numbers. Vincent, Martin and the whole gang rocked throughout the evening with some exciting rock and roll in jamming some more GV boppers like "Bluejean Bop" and "Woman Love." Gene and company also showed their love for Carl Perkins by performing his "Blue Suede Shoes."

At this particular performance I got to interview Gene.

BK: Gene how long have you been on the road and where are you going after this performance?

Gene: I have been on the road for several months now and have been touring the Midwest. We are scheduled to appear tomorrow night in Marysville, Kansas, for a record show and dance over there.

BK: Gene, how many gold records do you have to your credit?

Gene: I have sold over one-million copies in "Be-Bop-A-Lula" which has earned me a gold disc for that record.

BK: Do you have any favorite artists or styles of music that you enjoy listening to?

Gene: Yes, I enjoy what I am doing and love rock and roll very, very much. I also enjoy listening to Carl Perkins, Jerry Lee Lewis and Little Richard a whole lot. I love some forms of country music, but I cannot stand to hear that much jazz.

BK: Gene, what are your plans for the future?

Gene: I am planning on a tour of England after this tour at the end of this year. My records are picking up steam over there and they have requested for me to come visit the country and perform for my fans in Europe.

During the interview, Gene was very subdued, a little shy, but always friendly. He seemed to be a little bit on the gloomy side as if things weren't completely going right for him and that there was a lot to think about as if he was troubled. Gene's characteristics include being a bit modest, respectful and courteous through the entire visit with him. Gene finally politely excused himself and went back with someone else to his dressing room for final preparations to make the trip to Marysville, Kansas, for the next night's engagement.

It must be remembered that in 1959, Gene Vincent was already becoming a musical has-been because of the Philadelphia music scene picking up a lot of steam with such manufactured idols as Fabian, Frankie Avalon, and many others from other parts of the eastern seaboard that were dominating the charts during the last year of the fifties decade. During this year, Gene's career was relegated to small dances and record hops throughout the Midwest and the western part of the country since he didn't have any chart success nationally or even locally anywhere. This was most unfortunate because many of us found out in '59 that the Gene Vincent magic was still in tact in his vocality and performances. It was a shame that Gene couldn't be recognized more for the talents he still awesomely possessed during 1959 and the following years afterward. Gene was a magnificent rocker in every sense of the word.

Buddy Knox told a true story twenty-six years later about Gene. When he toured in 1959 with Gene and the Blue Caps, they were the wildest he had ever seen. "When I appeared in Miami, Florida, Gene and the Blue Caps literally wrecked the stage apart to the point that I couldn't go on. Eddie Cochran and me many times had to carry Gene off the stage because of his constant pains in his bad leg. I later booked Gene out of Minneapolis for some shows in Canada and the West."

When Gene Vincent passed away from ulcer problems due to over-drinking in 1971, I cried my heart out. His unfortunate death at his mother's home in California left many of his fans saddened and bewildered.

I agree with the statement Jerry Lee Lewis stated to me in 1969 about his old friend, Gene Vincent, and Gene's rightful status as a legendary rocker. "Everybody has tried to go pluck-pluck and play the guitar like Gene Vincent, but God bless him 'cause Gene is the greatest."

Gene Vincent's stature as a memorable rocker is unprecedented around the world. The late John Lennon admitted many times in the sixties that he has tried to copy the technique of phrasing and coloring a song lyric the way Gene used to style his recorded material. In France, Gene Vincent posthumously is a rock and roll superstar and is bigger than Elvis there with a devout fan club following that rivals anybody else's second to none. Gene was the very first rock star to have his own name enshrined on the Walk of Stars in Hollywood. The Teddy Boys in London, England still idolize him while Gene's original recordings continually get reissued in Great Britain as well as in France and the United States. The famed American disc jockey, Wolfman Jack, tributes Gene as being the one who "Pioneered white rock and roll." One of Gene Vincent's biggest Capital recordings help summarize in the song's title, what is still happening today by those fifties fanatics that are keeping his memory and recordings alive — he still is "The Bop That Won't Stop."

Rare pic's of Gene and the Blue Cap's 1959 St. Joseph, Mo. concert

TESTIMONY FROM A LEGENDARY GUITARIST

"—I played with them all—Little Richard, Roy Brown, Fats Domino, Don Covay, Chuck Willis," says Chuck Booker.

Chuck Booker may not be a household name, but if success for a musician is measured by the track record of a middle-aged black man who has played with the best of the early legends of rock and roll, both on stage and on vinyl, then Booker is a prime candidate for such an honor as a role model for other aspiring guitarists.

Chuck Willis, one of Booker's favorite artists, who was affectionately known as "The King of the Stroll" and "The Shiek of Rock and Roll." His career was very short-lived when his seemingly self-fulfilled prophecy became a stark and dark reality. Chuck Willis died on April 10, 1958, as a result of a brain tumor right after he had recorded his last two original hits for Atlantic in "Hang Up My Rock and Roll Shoes" and "What Am I Living For."

"I played with Chuck on many of his recording sessions," exclaimed Booker. "I was on "Hang Up My Rock and Roll Shoes" but I left Chuck just five months prior to his death. Chuck was a terrific guy and one of the easiest singers to accompany. he was a masterful song-writer who knew how to work with lyrics."

While singers like Chuck Willis was easy to get along with, there were some that weren't. "Dinah Washington was hard," admitted Chuck. "She was not very easy to get along with. If something wasn't right, she would stop right in the middle of a song in front of everyone on stage."

Chuck had an untold story to tell about an encounter he had with the rock instrumental guitar legend, Duane Eddy. A lot of song ideas are plagiarized by the artists themselves that they sometimes inadvertently got from someone else. Chuck's related story is certainly no exception. "After watching me perform several times, Duane (Eddy) invited me to come up to his apartment after my club appearance in Washington, D.C. He watched and listened as I played a tune he later recorded and had a hit in "Forty Miles of Bad Road."

Other studio sessions Booker mentioned that he had played on include Don Covay's "Have Mercy, Baby," and more recently, he has been recording as well as touring with the Clovers. Besides picking his red-colored Fender guitar for the Clovers, Booker has also cut a new record with the New Orleans-based rock legend Fats Domino. "We cut a follow-up unique answer to Lloyd Price's "Stagger Lee" with "The Trial of Stagger Lee."

Chuck's invaluable years of experience however has not been without some embarassing moments in the studio. In 1961, after an appearance at the Apollo Theatre, Chuck celebrated afterward but got inebriated. He had a scheduled recording session late that very night in New York with Barbara Mason. Chuck was playing so many mistakes on the session as a result of his delicate condition that the producers had to take his playing off of the recorded tracks.

Booker explains that musical trends isn't any better today, than say 1958-64, except the fact that the business end is now more efficient. "The music business today is better in the publishing and production end," claims Booker. "There is better promotion and contractual setups today, but thirty years ago, the bluesmen for instance wouldn't get paid for their recordings or got paid very little. Back then, promoting and also touring were the means to take advantage of plugging a new record. The artists did all the touring and usually the hard work but the companies got the benefits but not the artists themselves. I made one hundred and twenty dollars a night with having a number one record like in the Clover's "Love Potion Number Nine" hit in 1959. Actually, touring today is the catalyst for records while back then the records were the catalyst for the touring. Actually, the rock and roll shows were major events back in the fifties and sixties because they didn't happen just every day or every hour of the day like on television and everywhere else today."

After thirty years of recording and performing as an accompanist, it is obvious that Chuck today is happier than ever. He enjoys the stage and working with his friends, the Clovers which helps bring back the good old days of working together. Chuck Booker has backed the legends and near legends of rock and roll. Even though Chuck shows some facial lines, this talented guitarist with brisk blues overtones in his playing, still possesses a bright luster and sharply honed resilence in his endless hours of picking and performing for the public.

BIZARRE FANDOM

Since Elvis exploded on the record scene in 1956, there have been fan clubs, memorabilia, and all kinds of strange and exotic mementos of rock and roll recording stars for sale, ranging from the benign to the most bizarre.

For starters, Elvis fans may remember all the trinkets that were merchandised in 1957-'58, including the Elvis flash button and "Love Me Tender" penchants. There was even a musical box with "The Pelvis" shaking and jiggling to one of his tunes with a carnival background setting that matched the atmosphere projected in this nearly six-inch high gizmo.

Fabian Forte was one of the five possible heirs to Elvises vacant throne, during Presley's leave of absence in the Army. Fabian for a short while in the late fifties, shared the spotlight with Pat Boone, Frankie Avalon, Paul Anka, and RCA Records hopeful, Rod Lauren.

Fabian's good looks made his picture very marketable. In 1960, his young boyish charm was plastered on teenage girls' penchants, sold in department stores all across America. These pieces of jewelry not only had an oval-shaped picture of Fabe, but, also an original locket of his genuine hair!

Pat Boone's trademark of white buck shoes helped shoe company sales in the late fifties while Paul Anka's sweet ballads like "Diana" sold a lot of sheet music. Pat Boone wasn't the last one either to enhance shoe sales because Chubby Checker's cherry red twist shoes and the fashionable Beatle Boots popularized by the fearless foursome and Jerry Lee Lewis helped create a trend in footwear.

Beatlemania brought about enough collectables that could fill a book with such original 1964 items as life-size promotional store displays and even some pillows the Beatles slept on in a downtown Kansas City hotel room, were also sold on the auction block by some enterprising businessmen.

Back in 1960, some real fanatics decided to go after the scalp of singer, Rick Nelson. His fan club in Hollywood had made arrangements with a local barber to collect the hairs from the singer's supposedly highly prized scalp.

The most bizzare of what fan's will try and collect from their favorite rock singers, came in the late sixties when the Plaster Casters of Chicago would make actual real mantlepieces from the molds they would make of their favorite singer's privates.

Elvis Presley's death in August 17, 1977, sparked possibly the weirdest and most far out of items that were sold to keep his memory alive. The souvenir shops in and around Memphis had anything and everything for the Elvis fanatic to buy including Elvis marriage and driver's licenses to a copy of El's own will. The atypical Elvis freak could also purchase an Elvis thermo bottle, Elvis thermometers, Elvis decanters, Elvis enema's, and, believe it or not, a patented merchandised original one of a kind guaranteed item—Elvis' sweat!

It has never been unusual for rock and roll stars like their fans to fantasize. While their loyal followers will possess fantasies about going on a date or even to bed with his or her favorite idol, it is equally understandable to entertain the thought that rock and roll singers also have dreams and delusions of grandeur in various degrees.

In 1960, the late great Jackie Wilson dreamed of one day playing the lead acting role to his idol's life story—"I would like to do the "Al Jolson Story," he once said.

Rick Nelson at the height of his popularity in 1960, had sexual fantasies of being involved with his dream lady, a young aspiring British actress by the name of Joan Collins. The scandal sheets and gossip magazines in 1960 flaunted articles on Rick's passive desires toward Miss Collins.

One well known rock star from England that refuses to be identified, said that his fantasy is to be able to spend more time alone with a fifth of gin and a Playboy magazine craddled at his side.

Another British rock singer spends thousands of dollars in New York by living out his own fantasy of taking pictures (without film) of beautiful nude models posed in kinky positions.

In the last twenty-five years, a rare breed of rock and rollers have had their share of musical originality coupled with gadgets and gimmickry that are so outrageously different as if they were out of "Ripley's Believe It Or Not." For example, a cross sampling of rockdom's sideshow entertainers with their famous trademarks that at the time seem freaky by some standards like Jerry Lee Lewis' twenty-five pounds of marcelled blond hair, Carl Lee Perkins' Blue Suede

Shoes, Little Richard's zoot suits and pompadour hair style, Screamin' Jay Hawkins with his stage props including a skull and coffins, Elvis' sideburns, Paul Revere's revolutionary hats, Alice Cooper's snakes, Ozzy Osbourne's edible Bats, Arthur Brown's head of fire, and the list goes on.

If a gambling man would wager a bet that Percy Thrillington is the biggest recording star (worth over half a billion dollars) in the history of popular music, he would walk away with all the winnings. Thrillington recorded some orchestral works for Capitol Records in 1978. His half-animal, half-human features on the album's cover went virtually unnoticed and no more projects were ever followed up in the planning stages. What was Percy's real true name? — Paul McCartney!

Do-Wop king Lee Andrews from Philadelphia took his road show to even more limitless proportions in 1981 by adding a one of a kind dancer from the darkest corners of Jamaica to perform her death-defying flame act (hairy legs and all) by doing the Limbo under a flaming bar of fire which often at times put her less than a quarter of an inch away from certain death while Lee kept on singing his pleading ballad, "Try the Impossible."

Screaming Jay Hawkins for years since his fifties hit, "I Put A Spell on You" has been grinding away at zinging his fans especially in England with a VooDoo image. He portrays himself to be like a Witchdoctor or even a Zombie rising from the coffin with his favorite skull, Henry, as his constant companion. This grim scene was portrayed in the Film, "American Hot Wax" which was a movie biography on the life of Alan Freed.

It is really hard to predict which direction Bizarre Fandom will take in the future. Whether it would be Madonna's edible under panties or a wig of Dolly Parton's which would be auctioned to an investor or a collector, etc., those fans or even the artists themselves will chase after rock and roll dreams or personal momentos of their favorite idols.

PERCY THRILLINGTON

ROCK AND ROLL
EPITAPH

Buddy Holly, Richie Valens and The Big Bopper suffered untimely deaths when their small private aircraft dived and crashed into a pasture next to a fence near Clear Lake, Iowa. The trio was going to a teen dance at Moorehead, Minnesota after appearing at the Clear Lake Ballroom.

Waylon Jennings was in Buddy's band and flipped a coin with Richie Valens to see who was going to fly to Minnesota with Buddy. Valens won the toss and mentioned that he never won anything before. By the flip of the coin, fate was decided on who would live and who would die.

The snow storm caused the plane to fly with too much ice on the wings and tail. The plane nose-dived soon after take-off toward the ground at a speed of at least 250 miles per hour causing instant death for those aboard.

At the time of the tragedy, Richie Valens was having a top ten smash with "Donna" (named after his girlfriend, Donna Ludwig) and "La Bamba." He was being hailed and predicted to become the next biggest teen rage since Elvis. Valens' Mexi-Rock with its distinctive percussion rhythms was a highly infectious beat that caused the seats to empty at record hops across America.

Actually it was Richie Valens and not Buddy Holly that received the headline stories involving the crash. Also, Richie Valen's version of "Malaguenia" is a Flamingo acoustical guitar instrumental that has since become a standard for all pickers. One unique platinum, blond-haired picker in St. Joseph, Missouri, by the name of Cotton made "Malaguenia" his own Vehicle on a guitar he made out of his Oak tree in 1960.

Valens, just prior to the tour, had made his debut motion picture in "Go Johnny Go" whereas Holly never made any movie guest spots neither as an actor or an artist.

Paragraphs and paragraphs of accolades were directed toward Richie Valens including a published article in a popular teen magazine that was written by Valen's sweetheart, Donna Ludwig, who penned a public letter about how much Richie meant to her and how much she missed him.

An irony to all this was that Richie had a fear of flying from an incident nearly two years before his death. In June, 1957, Richie went to his grandfather's funeral instead of going to school at Pocalma' County Junior High. While he was away, a transport plane collided with a navy plane and the transport nose-dived into the school-ground, killing the crew and several of Richie's playmates—kids that he would have been with if he hadn't have gone to the funeral. To think that he would have been killed by a plane two years prior to his own instant death from a plane crash and the fact that Richie picked May 13th, 1958 as his lucky day, has a chilling effect on his life story.

The late DJ, Alan Freed said after the February 3rd tragedy that "It was a sad day for rock and roll. That Buddy Holly—we toured together for forty-four days. He was a bug for flying. Richie hated it. The Bopper just slept and didn't care one way or the other. But, Buddy—if you tied two orange crates together, put a string on it and said it would fly he'd climb in and take off. He always wanted to get some place ahead of the others."

Freed in 1959 continued his sadness of Buddy and the other's passing—"Crazy isn't it that his new hit is called " 'It Doesn't Matter anymore—'."

Alan on his TV Show asked a minute of silent prayer in memory of the three boys. Also, Roy Hamilton

paid a tribute to Holly, The Bopper and Richie by singing "You'll Never Walk Alone." Little did Freed or
Hamilton know that other artists just a few years later,
would also sing tributes to not only Holly, Valens and
the Bopper, but also to the late Alan Freed and the late
Roy Hamilton. It was mortally ironic that Freed and
Hamilton closed Alan's tribute show to the other three
immortals.

Buddy Holly had somewhat of a first revival of his
own music in 1963, when a number of his albums were
re-released on his label, Brunswick-Coral—The availabili-
ty of LP's by Holly were numerous including "The Great
Buddy Holly," "The Buddy Holly Story (volumes one and
two)" and "Reminiscing." The latter LP also featured the
Fireballs backup band that later had hits with "Sugar
Shack" and "Daisy Pedal Pickin'!" George Tomsco, the
Fireball's guitarist who wrote many of their hits, was also
a protégé of the late Norman Petty, who produced sessions for Holly, The Fireballs, and The Norman Petty
Trio, among others. In 1984, Tomsco, now writing, recording and performing out of Independence, Missouri,
recalled an interesting meeting between himself and Holly. "I went into Norman's studio and I saw this guy in
be-spectacled glasses playing and messing with my
guitar. I felt like a lot of other guys do and (felt) mad
and upset at somebody else messing with my instrument
without my permission. And, I felt I needed to be pro-
tective—So I asked Norman who is playing my guitar
and he said it was Buddy. He was a real gentleman so
I let him play it."

Dick Clark in an interview admitted that if Holly
would have lived, he sincerely doubted that Buddy
would have mastered his own publicity by staying in
music as a producer, and music publisher.

The belief that Buddy Holly was a major rock star
in 1959 is unfortunately a myth. Holly was struggling
and part of the reason that he accepted the fatal mid-
western tour that led to his pre-mature death.

His follow-up records in 1958-59 didn't sell in proportion to what "Peggy Sue" did for him in 1958 (actually, Buddy's Tex-Mex sound was more popular in 1980 than 1960, due to the release of "The Buddy Holly Story" starring Gary Busey).

It isn't every day that anyone hears about a rock and roll singer that has planned to will his organs to science after death.

One such singer that willed himself to benefit others was Bobby Darin.

Darin passed away on December 20, 1973 after being a victim of heart ailments that had plagued him throughout most of his life since rheumatic fever hit him at an early age. Darin had under-gone open heart surgery for the second time since 1971 to correct malfunctioning of two artificial heart valves. Unfortunately, the four skilled surgeons at the Cedars of Lebanon Hospital in Hollywood couldn't save Darin as he was "Just too weak to recover" from the six hour operation.

Darin was born Walden Robert Cassoto and hustled his way out of the Bronx to eventually become a millionaire by age 24. Bobby's night club and movie appearances earned him in excess of $2-million. Bobby Darin married his first leading lady, Sandra Dee shortly after completion of his first film, "Come September" in 1960.

His greatest awards include four gold records, two grammys and an Oscar nomination for his role in the flick "Captain Newman, M.D." Darin's own fantasy and direct goal was to surpass everything Frank Sinatra had accomplished in show business. "I hope to pass Frank in everything he's done," admitted Darin in his burning desire for further recognition.

Darin's first big year was 1958 when "Splish Splash," "Queen of the Hop" and "Plain Jane" topped the national charts. The songs bore the name of Bobby Darin, which he claimed to have gotten out of a phone book.

In 1959, Darin began reaching a more adult audience by cutting "Mack the Knife," a jazzy swing tune that was a parody of Louis Armstrong's style for Atco Records.

In 1966, Bobby Darin went into an entirely new direction by going electric folk-rock and made a brief comeback in the post-Beatle invasion period with Tim Hardin's "If I Were a Carpenter."

In the early seventies, Darin went into seclusion while growing his hair longer and wearing beads as he was moving closer to the Flower Children movement via Berkeley and San Francisco. Bobby still continually wrote songs and carried a cassette tape recorder with him in case a sudden idea came upon him. During the late sixties, Darin was desiring to record concept albums but his dreams in this area never fully materialized for him commercially.

Prior to his death, Bobby Darin instructed that his body be donated for medical research to the University of California, hoping that his service to mankind would help save the lives of others.

With a morbid sense of curiosity, there was an unexplainable twist of fate that precipitated a fatal car crash, and the wreck of a small plane into the hills of Tennessee, in the month of March in the year of 1962. Patsy Cline, Hawkshaw Hawkins, and Cowboy Copas were aboard that plane. They were flying back to Nashville from a Kansas City benefit performance for the late disc jockey, Cactus Jack Call, who was yet another victim that strangely the death jinx stalked and finally caught up with in yet another fatal accident—this time from an automobile mishap.

Before their bodies turned cold in their graves, another country music veteran, Jack Anglin, of the Johnny and Jack duo, died tragically in a single car crash while driving in transit to a prayer service at a local church for the late Patsy Cline.

Strange as it may seem, death actually struck soon once again on March 29, 1962, when Texas Ruby Owens, "The Sophie Tucker of Country Music" was burned to death in her trailer home.

The macabre specter of death that left its shocking marks on five talented victims in those last three weeks of only one month (March), left an ominous sign that is more coincidental and harder to believe and realize that the above facts even present. All three of the plane's casualties—Patsy Cline, Cowboy Copas, and Hawkshaw Hawkins had premonitions of death that were indirectly signaled and telegraphed in the lyrics of their last releases. "Don't leave me here in a world filled with dreams—" were part of the words in Miss Cline's last Decca recording, "Leavin' On Your Mind." Hawkshaw Hawkins had among his hits the prophetic "Bad News Travels Fast," while Cowboy Copas could have had premonitions of his own demise from the title of his last recording—"Goodbye Kisses."

It was ten-fifteen at Gene Banta's Golden Slipper in Village Green, Pennsylvania, on September 20, 1970, when Lloyd Arnold was working his way into his second set when he proceeded to fall against the front stage railing suffering from a drunken stupor. "I would like to sing "Hank William's Guitar" recorded by Freddie Hart," he lamented. Lloyd later finishes up the hour with a medley of his idol—Hank Williams' greatest hits like "I Can't Help It" and "Cold, Cold Heart."

Lloyd and his group, the Rockin' Drifters proceeded to take a twenty minute break whereby he quietly approaches the bar, as he busily straightens his dress coat and brushes it off while ordering another round of straight shots of Calvert whiskey.

Lloyd Arnold (real last name is McCullough) liberally brags and flaunts himself to anybody close at hand that would listen to him.

"I was one of the original Memphis rockers," admits Lloyd. "I could have recorded for Sun, but went with Meteor instead," he says.

"I knew them all—Carl Perkins, Bill Monroe, Jerry Lee Lewis, Elvis, Charlie Feathers—all of 'em. I played with Elvis on the Louisiana Hayride and was working for him 'till Red West took my place in El's chain of command.' "

"I went about things the wrong way. I had a chance to sign a contract with the Chicago White Sox, but started singing in my idol's (Hank Williams) footsteps instead. I should have done it all the opposite way and gotten into sports first and then it could have led me into a better music career like say, Conway Twitty. I was also in the Roller Derby in the fifties and was good at it too."

The Golden Slipper was a notorious bar that was only about ten miles from Philadelphia, which was Lloyd's home away from home. The fans that came out to see Lloyd at the Slipper, abandoned him as the Calvert Whiskey began to control and completely take over his life.

During Lloyd's appearances at the Golden Slipper, just a half a mile down the street at Jack Hurley's was this establishment's world famous house band in Bill Haley's Comets, featuring Ruby Pompelli on sax and guitarist, Nick Masters. Every now and then, the Comets would visit Lloyd at the Golden Slipper and a jam session would soon get under way.

Lloyd Arnold's early recordings are now much sought after collector's items including his "Red Coat, Green Pants, and Red Suede Shoes" that was released on the Philadelphia-based Myers label. This record is now worth well over eighty dollars to rockabilly collectors. Lloyd also cut "Sugaree" on Memphis Records and always claimed that he was the original singer of this song which he felt should give him rock and roll immortality. Lloyd and his group went under the name of the Longhairs in 1964, on the strength of the Beatles invasion and parodied the group on Chuck Berry's "Go, Go, Go," also released on Memphis.

In 1971, Lloyd found some financial backers in Delaware and with some money, he recorded on the K-Ark label, an LP of some of his very own favorites including "My Bucket's Got a Hole In It" and "School Days." Elvis Presley's former drummer, D. J. Fontana was one of Lloyd's session men.

Lloyd Arnold's last recorded venture occurred in late 1971, when he traveled to Oklahoma City and cut one of is own compositions in "What Can I Say." The late bass player for Conway Twitty—Joe Lewis, produced the session, just three years before he got killed in an automobile accident.

Lloyd tried for over fifteen years to find the right ingredients for a hit record. In retrospect, Lloyd was a paradox. He wanted on one hand to be recognized as a great star. On the other hand, he couldn't handle the idea of achieving any kind of success at all. He feared the so-called "big time," and in a subconscious way, held himself back by drinking to excess.

Lloyd became agonized and torn from a broken marriage that ended in divorce, and turned to countless affairs as a means of solace. Even a second marriage in the early seventies didn't save him from himself. Also, his alcoholism left him a miserable wreck with no way out. He finally found a way out for himself by ending it all with a shotgun. He blew his own brains out at his Memphis home in 1976.

Lloyd Arnold lived up to his favorite saying clear up to the bitter end—"Money talks and bullshit walks."

After Elvis Presley's tragic death, there were many of his fans holding on to the belief that Elvis didn't pass on, but wanted to lead a more personal life, so he threw this publicity stunt. They believed that Elvis Presley's body in the coffin on display at Graceland was actually a wax replica. A well known rockabilly singer along with others have believed that Elvis retired to an isolated ranch in New Mexico, to live in seclusion with Buddy Holly, Jim Morrison, and Marilyn Monroe.

Sam Cooke had one of the biggest rhythm ballads ever to hit the charts in "You Send Me" for the Los Angeles-based Specialty label back in 1957.

Sam and fellow vocalist, Lou Rawls, had an ironic twist of fate when they both cheated death while touring together in 1958, from a serious car accident that resulted in Rawls being in a coma for five-and-a-half days prior to fully recovering. Cooke eventually became a superstar in the late fifties and early sixties, while Rawls had to struggle a little longer before his talent was finally recognized to the extent that it is today.

In retrospect, it was Sam Cooke and a small handful of gospel-inspired singers that helped open the door for other blacks in a field dominated by caucasians.

In early 1960, Cooke moved over to RCA Victor, and his string of hits soon began, starting with "Chain Gang," right on through to "Shake" in January 1965.

Cooke, a dynamic showman with charisma to match, headlined "The Biggest Show of Stars for 1963" along with Dion (Dimucci) as his co-star.

Dee Clark was also a featured entertainer on this '63 bill related the story years later that "Dion felt that he should have been the headliner of the show." During his candid remarks, Dee also admitted that "Sam and him always got along." Clark clearly reminisced that the two of them always respected each other's talents as a rule in spite of Dion's personal feelings of professional jealousy. "When you travel and do thirty-six shows non-stop like we did in those days, you do become a family and get to know each other rather well," admits Dee. "Sam was the greatest and there is no way Dion could have taken the top spot away from him. I knew Sam Cooke back when he was still singing gospel music with the Soul Stirrers in Chicago," Dee said proudly.

Sam was an exhilarating performer. He would smoothly step out on stage in his brown leather hush puppy shoes, brown slacks and white-tailored shirt as his distinguished looking grey-haired manager would proudly gaze at Sam at the edge of stage left while also acting as body guard and keeping some of the screaming female admirers perched close by from coming on stage and grabbing and pulling at his clothes. Cooke would energetically work every corner of any large auditorium stage while dancing and weaving in and out of his songs with such flawless ease. For an encore, Sam Cooke and the rest of the entire entourage of the rock and roll extravaganze would in procession come on stage and close the show with Cooke leading the way for everyone to sing "Having A Party" (Dion wouldn't go back on with the rest of the performers). It was a classic and memorable moment to see on stage at one time such luminaries as Rai Donner, B. B. King, Dionne

Warwick, Dee Clark and Bobby "Blue" Bland grooving with each other dancing arm in arm with one another, while Little Willie John often taking front stage center was twisting, bobbing and shaking his hips all around next to Cooke while Sam gleefully watched Willie John's gyrations with an expression of approval shining on his face (None of them were obviously aware that this would be the very last time these particular artists would ever appear together).

In a 1964 interview, Sam Cooke felt that the way a singer phrases a song is an important aspect of the art of vocalizing and this facet has helped define his own style. Cooke also credited Nat King Cole and Frank Sinatra as his big influences.

In the last twenty years, other singers have been influenced one way or another by the Sam Cooke formula of crooning. Lou Rawls recognizes Cooke's effect on his own music and Joe Simon has also felt that Sam Cooke touch in his own vocal interpretations. Recently, Steve Perry of Journey has now taken up Cooke's smooth textured vocalizing.

Sam Cooke's tragic death is clouded in controversy. On the night of December 10, 1965, Cooke a married man picked up an oriental woman in a Los Angeles night club where he was singing. He took her, allegedly against her will, to a motel where he left the young girl in a rented room where he supposedly tried to rape her. She escaped and hid in a phone booth. Sam ran after her dressed with just an overcoat on his back and frantically broke into the apartment where he mistakenly thought the girl had run to. Sam had a vicious fight with the motel owner, a middle-aged lady by the name of Bertha Franklin. She picked up a twenty-two caliber pistol and started shooting. Cooke screamed in pain and agony that he was shot and he ran toward the lady again and she testified to police later that she fired the gun at Cooke one more time—"I (also) grabbed a stick. The first time I hit him it broke." This was partially the coroner's account of how Cooke's death came about.

It is entirely possible that one could question the accuracy of this account of Sam Cooke's tragic demise.

Because of Cooke's deepening involvement in the music industry there has been some of Sam's associates speculating that his murder was a mob killing—a set up.

Bobby Vinton in a magazine article dealing with Sam Cooke's death, spoke in defense of Sam and also admittedly pointed out the hardships, duress, and pitfalls of being an established popular singing star and how the many strenuous hours of life on the road can make anyone lose sight of themselves and untimately lose persective on life itself.

Other violent crimes that are related to rock and roll stars include rhythm and blues legend Johnny Ace mortally wounding himself in Texas where he was found dead backstage at a Christmas show as a result of playing Russian Roulette and paying the ultimate price by losing. Little Willie John's stabbing of an inmate in the Washington State Penitentiary came only just a short period before he died himself as a result of pneumonia. Shep Sheppard of Shep and the Limelights died on a cold New York subway from being beaten and stabbed to death. This was one of the saddest moments ever as Shep was one of the greatest tenor voices in Do-Wop history. Larry Williams who had such evergreens as "Boonie Maronie" and "Short Fat Fanny" was also a suicide victim leaving a life that was filled with over-zealous activities in sex and drugs.

Little Esther Phillips had a distinguished career of being an untiring torch singer whose voice is as distinctive as the vocality of the late Dinah Washington and Sarah Vaughn.

Miss Phillip's biggest hits were spawned from her obscure King-Federal days out of the fifties and her evergreens occurred far and between in the sixties and seventies. After her version of the country classic, "Release Me" made the charts in the early sixties, it took over seventeen years before Esther's next commercial success was achieved with her disco version of Dinah Washington's "What a Difference a Day Makes." The album from the hit single displayed a cover pose of Esther cradling and holding a fifteen foot long Boa Constrictor.

The Vine Street Bar and Grill is just a stone's throw off Hollywood and Vine and has been a haven for jazz and even rhythm and blues stylists. The nightly attractions there reads like a who's who of jazz oriented scat singers including Della Reese, Ruth Brown and the temptuous Esther Phillips.

Miss Phillips has built a solid following at this Vine Street venue through many personal appearances at this locale. During the latter part of March, 1984, Esther made yet another sparkling showing in front of a sell-out audience. The room at the Vine Street Bar and Grill is no bigger than two oversized john's but the gathering there was overly enthusiastic for Esther's two sets. (The men's room located just to the back-side of the band contains graffiti that validates the keen interest of this unique room's patron's for their favorite music—jazz. One such etching had an inscription right above the urinal which prolifically says, "When you fall asleep, don't count sheep, Count Basie."

With a three piece combo providing squeaky clean precisioned backing for Miss Phillip's finely tuned voice, her perennial performance that March night was among her best.

During the last few minutes of Esther's first set, a bar gigalo stationed at the bar was hounding one of the bartenders for a glass of water for Esther. This blond-haired gentleman made the mistake of demanding the refreshment instead of asking for it. The server fixed his hand on him and exclaimed, "Hey, the next time you talk to me that way again in that tone of voice, I'll throw you right out of here." After there was an ex-change of dirty stares, the wiry gentleman turned around and watched Esther and quipped, "Esther is a genius."

When Esther retired to the back room of the club, she was all wrapped up in a warm blanket from shiver-ing in her cold flesh from top to bottom as if she was freezing to death even though the temperature therein was warm. She was giving off dirty glances at people coming into the room with a firm statement—"I can't talk now." The irony of it all was that the bad leech at the bar was sitting in this secluded area close to her with his hand on hers. Just a few minutes earlier, he almost got bounced out of the bar and yet he seemed to be the only invited party backstage to sit with Esther.

In just a moment later, Esther was stumbling around the bandstand near the bar trying to find an earring she had lost during her night's performance. She frantically looked under a cushioned seat in a booth close to where she was singing at earlier and finally located the missing piece of jewelry there. She then quickly left the premises as fast as a bat of an eyelash. Anyone could sense that something was wrong because she not only looked worn and exhausted from a haggard physical appearance but also had a worried expression on her face as if Esther had a horrible premonition.

The epilogue to the above is unfortunately tragic. Esther Phillips died just a short time later of cirrhosis of the liver. This marked the final chapter of another life that was short lived and snuffed out as a result of hard living due to the harsh lifestyle of a truly brilliant lady.

A whole book can actually be written on the tragic premature deaths of rock singers. Marvin Gaye was murdered by his father; Danny Rapp, former lead vocalist of Danny and the Juniors ("At The Hop"—"Rock and Roll Is Here To Stay") committed suicide in Arizona; Jimi Hendrix and Janis Joplin died within two weeks of each other in September, 1970, to a death wish that made them both self-destructive from messing with an overdose of drugs.

Of all the great rock stars that have passed on including such early pioneers as Bill Haley, Gene Vincent, British rocker—Billy Fury, Elvis, Richie Valens, the Big Bopper and Buddy Holly, there is only one singular individual who died just before his career peaked and that was Eddie Cochran. Eddie was killed from traveling in a car that skidded into a lamp post on April 17, 1960. This rock and roll star from Albert Lee, Minnesota, was touring Great Britain when the mishap occurred. He died in Somerset Hospital in Bath, England. Eddie's fiancee, songwriter Sharon Sheeley and fellow artist and friend, Gene Vincent were both passengers in the car at the time of the accident also, but neither of them sustained any serious injury except Gene's badly wounded left leg from the early fifties motorcyle accident was further hampered from this wreck that made life even more unbearable for Gene to survive in.

Could Eddie's death actually been foretold in the studio? His posthumous last hit was "Three Steps to Heaven."

Although his rising stardom wasn't fully understood or appreciated in the states, the British was ecstatic about Eddie. It is rumored that ex-Beatle George Harrison followed him around England in 1960 and the BBC (British Broadcasting Company) aired a prime time documentary film on the life and times of Eddie Cochran that was aired in 1983.

The late John Lennon was also a great rocker a la 1959. While appearing at the Cavern in Liverpool, England in 1962, John and the rest of the Beatles were serving up some of the best rock and roll Great Britain ever had to offer. After the Beatles broke up in the early seventies, John re-discovered his roots once again by cutting a "Rock and Roll" album for Capitol of some of his favorite personal selections including the grinding rocker "Be Bop A Lula" and the soulful Ben E. King classic, "Stand By Me."

John Lennon always espoused a profound reverence for many of the top rhythm and blues and rockabilly singers who made their mark in the late fifties and early sixties. In 1964, John proclaimed that Earl Bostic (instrumental saxophonist for King Records) was his favorite instrumentalist with his musical tastes also leaning toward Chuck Jackson, Chuck Berry, Little Richard, Mary Wells, the Marvelettes, Chiffons, Miracles, Carl Perkins, Gene Vincent and the Shirelles. John once explained that many of the Beatle's early original compositions were particularly geared toward a more rhythm and blues feel. "PS I Love You" was meant to be a Shirelles kind of song," said Lennon.

John Lennon was also flattered when rhythm and blues vocalists recorded Lennon-McCartney tunes. John was simply amazed when the Fatman from New Orleans cut "Everybody's Got Something To Hide"—"Fats Domino did a great version of this one," professed Lennon. Even Roy Orbison had an influence on the Beatles. Songs like "Please, Please Me" were written via the Orbison style— "I wrote all of this one," admitted Lennon,"—I was trying to do a Roy Orbison." John was also influenced by Gene Vincent. His high pitched vocal phrasing technique was quickly picked up by the late chief Beatle and John later paid tribute to Gene by recording Vincent's timeless rocker, "Be Bop A Lula."

It's an entertaining thought that John Lennon is now jamming with Gene Vincent in Rock and Roll Heaven.

DRUGS, SEX, VIOLENCE AND
ROCK AND ROLL EUPHORIA

Artistry in rhythm has not only involved the musical aspects of rock, but the game of sex as well. The so-called groupie movement—those blind unquestionable followers of rock stars, who seem to have erotic fantasties of grandeur for their hairy heroes. Attitudes like "I would go out with anyone that's a musician," or "Since you're a drummer, I'll bet you are good in bed since you've got a whole lot of rhythm," have molded further orgasmic wet dreams.

The notorious Plaster Casters in the late sixties validated this feeling that rock entertainers would and could be actually exploited in more ways than the number sixty-nine would even indicate.

Since recorded music was especially made for erotic sex sirens and strippers (also known as exotic dancers) in the fifties and sixties with such titles as "For Strippers Only," "How To Strip For Your Husband," "Belly Dancing For Your Husband," etc., these concept type of albums opened up some of the more sensual aspects of popular music. David Rose's "The Stripper" helped marry even further the two themes of sex and contemporary music.

Actually, sex has always had a subliminal tie with rock. Born out of the risqué bars and burlesque houses and honky tonks in the twenties, thirties, forties, and fifties, such songs like Hank Ballard's "Annie Had A Baby" to "Sixty Minute Man" by Billy Ward and the Dominoes in the mid-fifties had sexual overtones to them. These early rhythm and blues offerings were designed as audience participation dance numbers that contained hidden messages and meanings that were partially disguised by a dominating beat. "Louie, Louie" is an example of a controversial song whereby the lyrics were supposedly vulgar, but the beat was so strong that nobody could understand what the lead singer of the Kingsmen was saying.

Today, nothing is actually hidden or left to the imagination. The twenty-four hour music channel of hard rock—MTV, and the Playboy Channel, lets everyone bare it all to the point where there is nothing left to imagine. Playboy has aired "The Girls of Rock and Roll." These sultry rock videos contain plenty of nudity and sexuality. If the video revolution occurred in the fifties, it would have been harder to conjure up a video to a song like Hank Ballard's "Annie Had A Baby." The music trends in the fifties had some sexual connotations to them, but there were no videos around at the time to pollute an already wet imagination.

Eventually, certain songs throughout the last twenty years have gotten more and more explicit in nature such as "Teach Me Tiger" and "Love To Love You Baby."

Even Porno-Queens got into the act by crossing over into popdom. As a classic example, Marilyn Chambers, "The Ivory Snow Girl" turned blue girl of porn, sang a sex-oriented song for a campaign promotional giveaway for a well known men's magazine a few years ago. Her lips-shaped cardboard disk was a bonus freebie to buyer's of the tabloid.

Sex and Violence have an uncanny relationship with rock and roll. The human libido was aroused in 1956 when Elvis shook and wiggled his way into teenage America. He was transfixed in our minds as something that was truly overpowering. Only Frank Sinatra, Johnny Ray, Marilyn Monroe, and James Dean (the latter two were recording artists also) preceded Elvis as a sexual image that was dominate in size and dimension that made the public view them as gods in both autistic art-forms and film and music.

In a more serious vein, after Marlon Brando's gang bang film about biker's that rumble and rape in "The Wild One's," an all-girl motorcycle gang was rampaging and terrorizing the countryside north of Kansas City in 1958. It was reported by all news accounts that these savage ladies of death and doom would perform hedonistic rituals with details that would spook your local chapter of "Hell's Angels." These fearsome ladies would become beasts of the night by kidnapping young males and castrating them in wooded areas located around Northwest Missouri while strains of "Great Balls of Fire" would be screaming from the gang's portable radios. The reported occurrences struck fears into the hearts of the young as vicious rumors and counter rumors were held to a maximum.

The rock and roll shows of the early sixties made headlines not because of the staged presentations, but as a direct result of activity off the stage in the form of gang fights and riots. Bill Haley and the Comets got caught up in the middle of mass rioting in their first English tour in 1957. Their arrival in Great Britain created more news coverage and pandemonium than even the Beatles mustered in the early sixties there.

Some of the riots during rock and roll shows in 1959 were actually more pronounced in scope than the more hyped type of notorious rioting of any Alan Freed revues.

Thus, the early rock and roll shows were more than just the name implies—they were real happenings that only occurred on an average of only three to four times a year. Supersonic Attractions out of Chicago was the booking agency that often supported such an event that usually featured the top rock and rollers anywhere including Clyde McPhatter, Brook Benton, Jackie Wilson, Sam Cooke, Jerry Lee Lewis. Chuck Berry and Bo Diddley. General Artists Corporation based in Milwaukee, Wisconsin, booked many of the top stars into different venues all over North America. Several different theatres also booked through their respective management the number one mommies and daddies from coast to coast. The Schiffman family who managed Harlem's Apollo Theatre in New York City, would feature on any given night a headliner such as Chuck Jackson with other recording stars in attendance looking on in the audience including the Rolling Stones and Tom Jones.

Alongside such concert stages as the Royal Theatre, Chicago's Regal, The Howard in Washington not to mention the Hollywood Bowl, there were many smaller venues that equally as well showcased the premier talent of the late fifties and early sixties. For example, in Kansas City, Genova's Chesnut Inn offered its bar crowd on any given night the cream of the crop from the rockabilly and country field such as Jerry Lee Lewis, Willie Nelson, Roy Clark, the Collins Kids, Wanda Jackson, Hank Thompson, Conway Twitty, Ernest Tubb, George Jones, and Charlie Rich. Charlie Genova, the club's owner, reported in 1962 that George Jones was his best draw while Charlie Rich was lucky to play in front of five people in spite of his hit of "Lonely Weekends" and the release he was promoting in 1961—"Mountain Dew."

While Elvis was filming "Blue Hawaii" in cozy comfort, Jerry Lee Lewis would be putting his life into his own hands by playing in a white segregationist bar like Genova's, centered geometrically like a time bomb in the middle of a black populated area of town where race riots have occurred. Charlie Genova was an ardent segregationist who candidly told the local blacks that they were not asked in his establishment, even if they were striving to enter or needed a drink of water. Charlie Genova fought hard for his convictions clear up to the steps of city hall and ultimately to the Supreme Court. He fought long and hard against the 1964 Civil Rights movement, but of course lost the battle when then President Lyndon Johnson signed it into law. While all of this transpired, Jerry Lee Lewis just kept on rockin'.

In just a short distance away from Genova's Chesnut Inn, there was another popular hot night spot also on Twelfth Street and Vine called the Orchid Room. This bar was three hundred and sixty degrees different than Genovas in that this small lounge supported such nightly revues that would feature the Ravens, LaVerne Baker, the Drifters and sultry strippers would also help augment the entertainment such as Black Velvet. The Orchid hosted the top black rhythm and blues recording singers from the early to late fifties before it finally met its demise in the sixties.

On the other side of the coin, a big packaged program was always something to look forward to. A two dollar and fifty cent ticket holder to such an occurrence would see rock and roll history in the making — Gene Chandler and James Brown's caped collapse routines, Sam Cooke's gliding showmanship and melodic phrasings of songs, Jackie Wilson's eye-popping splits, spins and back-flips and Dee Clark's sweating twists and turns and even more entertainment that would boggle the imagination.

The predominately black rock and roll shows of the fities and early sixties were real gems. The four hour

spectaculars would first open with a fifteen piece orchestra complete with horns, keyboards and a rhythm
section with all of them (including the drummer) reading
charts. For the first hour, the entourage would warm up
the audience with some intricate but hot traditional
mixed with progressive-styled two-four, and four-four
tempo jazz selections with progressive overtones whereby
different soloists from the orchestra (usually a Lloyd
Price, Paul "Hucklebuck" Williams, B. B. King or Bobby
"Blue" Bland aggregation) would step up stage center to
the microphone and play his selected parts. Whether it
would be a saxophonist or a trumpet player, all the
musicians on these revues would make Chuck Mangione
or most of today's musicians look and sound like begin-
ners. These unknown artists would make themselves very
known throughout the duration of an evening's performance. For example, during a 1963 soul tour with
Chuck Jackson and Jerry Butler, the late Jimi Hendrix
worked on this bill and he would amaze the rock and
roll crowds with his ear-piercing blues licks which included Jimi sawing off notes by plucking the strings of
his Fender guitar with his teeth. Sometimes these big
bands would carry more than one percussionist and
drummer. There would be on occasion three drummers
with each one socking the skins and cymbals with
blistering accentuated drum licks or they would play
synchronized lightning fast single-double stroke rolls and
paradiddles with quick accuracy.

The patrons (usually eighty to ninety percent of the
audiences were black with the remaining ten to twenty
percent being either of Mexican or caucasian ancestry)
would come dressed in formal, flashy and colorful attire
to all these shows and treat the affairs like get together's
to a high school reunion or a family picnic. There

would be much hand shaking and back slapping of arms and hands while different friends and acquaintances would get some group shots by another friend or family member who is taking pictures with his or her new Polaroid camera. Everybody would circulate and mill around with different people, always talking and sometimes renewing old friendships.

The black women would wear comely dresses that would accent their breathtaking figures. There was one woman at one of the Kansas City shows that wore a very low-cut bright red shiny evening gown just touching her forty-two-D breasts with the bottom of her skin-tight dress heightened way above her calves with a wide slit that came completely up to her size thirty-eight hips. The lady's spiked red-colored high heels and matching red wide-brimmed hat helped make this black sex siren's six foot movie star frame stand out even more.

On the other hand, the men were dressed in their sometimes loud and flashy Zoot suits matched up with fancied feather hats with a varied assortment of colors from bright blues to passionate pinks.

After a fifteen minutes intermission (usually the duration of which lasted thirty minutes or longer because they knew that no one was going to leave, especially with the likes of Jackie Wilson or Chuck Jackson headlining the bill), the emcee, usually a comedian in the person of Harold Cromer (who was once LaVerne Baker's Jim Dandy) or Arnold Dover would entertain the crowd for about ten minutes, telling racial jokes about white people or making fun at themselves. They may even relate an amusing experience that might have occurred backstage with Jackie Wilson, for instance. In another example, Harold Cromer once announced Bruce

Channel (a pop singer from Texas who was having a hit in 1962 with "Hey Baby" and was making his first national appearance on "The Biggest Show of Stars For 1962—Spring Edition") to the stage and proclaimed to the chuckling gathering that "Bruce is the only colored man in the show" as Bruce is white and the rest of the cast were black.

Just prior to startime, the orchestra would once again heat up the audience with such scorchers as "Sidewinder" and even a complex tune that's played in a five-four time signature like "Take Five" would be included in the evening's offerings.

All of the acts (including the headliners) would do three to six numbers each (including their current hits of the time) and then give way to the other artists that were still awaiting backstage to make an appearance. To illustrate the above, Gladys Knight and the Pips would do their hit, "Every Beat Of My Heart" followed by a leggy hip shaking Barbara George would follow on stage and strut her stuff with two more selections and then finish up the grinding set with her then recent hit offering, "I Know."

Unfortunately, some of the stars the fans came to see would either perform very little or not even show up for the concert at all. The former statement was very much evident when Eddie Cochran co-starred with Billy Ward and the Dominos and Jerry Lee Lewis for "The Biggest Shower of Stars for 1958." He only sang about three offerings including "C'Mon Everybody" and "Summertime Blues." In another contrast, Supersonic Attractions had yet another tour package—"The Battle of the Century"—Jackie Wilson versus Jerry Lee Lewis that criss-crossed the Midwest in October, 1961. At the Kansas City date, these two principals didn't bother to show up. It was announced that Jackie and Jerry Lee were involved in a car wreck as a result of rainy slick pavement they encountered in Columbia, Missouri on their way to the Kansas City concert date.

On a mild Saturday night in Kansas City in October, 1959, racism and violence were to bump heads one more time in what was to become one of the most violent incidents in that city's history. When this all-star roadshow, The Dick Clark Caravan of Stars got to this mid-western cowtown, a sell-out audience of nearly twelve thousand people came out in masse to see LaVerne Baker, Duane Eddy, Annette, the Coasters, Lloyd Price, the Skyliners, Phil Phillips, the Jordan Brothers, Bobby Rydell, the Drifters, Jimmy Clanton and Paul Anka.

When sultry LaVerne Backer in her sparkling figure fitting one piece gown was grinding out "Tweedle Dee" during her set, a dangerous explosive situation erupted on the near center arena floor when a band of youths set off a large fireworks display in a very over-crowded arena floor. The explosive fireworks crackled with loud bangs that shook the arena, causing people to panic and flee out of the building. The firecrackers caused a chain reaction of events including one innocent bystander getting stabbed in the stomach and another rock fan was shot and had to be rushed to a nearby hospital.

While walking down a narrow hallway corridor, I was attacked by three blacks with one of them slamming my portable camera off my shoulders onto the concrete floor. But, the over-zealous fan came back and picked the camera up and made sure I was alright and sincerely apologized for his impulsive aggressive behavior.

As Lloyd Price was singing with his own aggregation, the Lloyd Price Orchestra, who backed most of the other entertainers, brought many couples dancing in the aisles. Lloyd was performing Ray Charles' "What'd I Say" when a young dark-haired male youth, sporting a long-ducktail and turtle-neck sweater, seated near the top rows on the south end of the arena, stood up and began a hip shaking dance a la Elvis that had caught the attention of several-hundred hysterical female bystanders near this impromptu performer's side of the upper balcony, and half the arena crowd was looking on.

The rock and roll patrons were overly hyper by the time crooner Paul Anka hit center stage. This headliner would crumble to his knees and kiss several swooning young female teens who were crunched together around the stage.

When Paul Anka did hit the stage, a lot of rowdies were hitting at each other. After more than one fracus erupted, the police brought in several ambulances and paddy wagons to arrest troublemakers and to aid the victims of the attackers.

"Quell Teen Brawl At Dance In Arena"—this was the front page headline in the Sunday, October 18, 1959 edition of the Kansas City Star. The Star reported that the teen brawl had to be stopped by the city's police riot squad. Police took three paddy wagons full of those arrested back to police headquarters to be interrogated and booked. One youth reportedly had fired a twenty-two caliber revolver from the balcony. When a police-man ran toward the gunman, he ran and lost himself in the crowd who were packed in the arena like sardines. It took about fifty officers to dissipate the enormous gathering at this rock and roll spectacular.

The press account of the evening's incidents at the arena were diverse and many—.

"One guy got his glasses knocked off and was swinging blindly at anything that moved."

"Although auxiliary police and special auditorium of-ficers were on duty, it took a night-stick-swinging group of police reinforcements to bring the mob into order."

"One man who was even seen in a rest room had one arm and a fifth of whiskey in a sling."

"Police reported finding some men in women's rest rooms when the building was cleared."

"Five police officers carried one man from the auditorium to a patrol wagon. He was kicking and biting and tried to kick officers after being taken to head-quarters."

"One woman who frantically came to the auditorium and tried to enter pleading, 'Please let me in. I want to get my daughter out of there.' "

But the throng was so heavy, she was shoved out to the sidewalk."

David Booker who booked the show said, "I don't know nutten about nutten 'till I saw the policemen coming in here. One little incident caused the whole thing. Somebody called the riot squad down. It was entirely unnecessary."

Dancing was to follow the performance, but the disturbance caused it to be cancelled.

This concert was banned from going to Omaha, Phoenix and other cities as a result of the Kansas City riot which caused a stir among the national press corps and was condemned and criticized by mayors from several municipalities as being a vulgar form of enter-tainment that also promotes juvenile delinquency.

Dick Clark and his co-producer of the "Caravan" tour, Irving Feld (he later owned Barnum and Bailey's "Greatest Live Show On Earth" circus) steadfastly denied that rock and roll itself was to blame for the distur-bances or that the music itself is in any way responsible for public violence.

There are other acts of violent rioting that followed.

Trouble followed James Brown around in the early to mid-sixties. Mr. Brown's brand new bag was not just his papa's but also his own. His October, 1962, "Live At The Apollo" LP for King Records was so compelling that upon listening to this release, anyone could actually see the sweat dripping off the vinyl. When he beckoned his audience to "Try Me," the girls shrieked and screamed at him in hopes to do just that. Whether Mr. Brown's fans were married or not really didn't matter—in the heat of the moment, they wanted him.

It is well documented that James Brown's staged productions would work his crowds into a frenzy, from the cape routines that included falling to his knees in agonized simulated painful mercy pleadings in the gospel-inspired "Please, Please, Please" to his wicked but dazzling visually blurred dance variations that would be displayed on such songs as "I Got Ants In My Pants." James would create mass hysteria and even riots while warbling "Sexy, Sexy, Sexy" to testifying on "I Lost Someone."

"Uncle" Walter Cronkite on the CBS Evening News reported a riot at a James Brown concert in Kansas City on Thanksgiving, 1966, when the revue erupted into a full scale free for all. People started pushing and shoving each other on the arena floor in the KC Auditorium. People panicked as friends were turned into foes as everyone on the main floor battled it out and threw everyone and everything in sight at each other making people and bottles into lethal weapons of warfare. Switchblade knifes and guns were drawn as the metro police came into the maddening scene to quell the hostility by unleashing German Shepherd attack dogs. Needless to say, this maneuver quickly dissipated the rowdy patrons. The swat-styled police team had the arena under control in just a matter of a few minutes. Several fans had suffered injuries and many ambulances took them away to nearby hospitals. Many paddy wagons were brought in to handle all of those that were arrested.

L. D. Williams was a tenor saxophonist that worked for James Brown's orchestra in the sixties and who now lives in Los Angeles, described in vivid detail that fateful Thanksgiving evening over twenty years ago. "—I was there when the riot was on too. I'll tell you what I remember about it you know—the band was playing and James Brown was going on with his show. And myself, I play with my eyes shut all the time, you know, and I just heard a rumble like an earthquake and I looked up and saw all those people just fighting and a lot of running going on. I left out the back entrance and went to the downtown and didn't go back."

Upon hearing about this disturbance that erupted in this usually quiet midwestern city, other municipalities that already had the review booked such as Omaha cancelled out the James Brown tour.

The irony of it all is that when racial tension occurred in 1968 as a result of Civil Rights leader, Dr. Martin Luther King's assassination, it was James Brown that helped lead the way in helping the authorities keep the peace by stopping widespread street violence and racial tension.

Another dramatic night that came very close to terminating my own life happened at yet another rock and roll spectacular in the Kansas City Auditorium. Just before the concert started that starred Jerry Butler, an enraged woman who discovered her boyfriend escorting another lady friend decided to terminate them both. Perched far into the second balcony on the east side of the venue, she was unfortunately able to spot and locate the careless couple arriving. As they were walking south on the east side of the arena floor toward the stage, she flew into an uncontrollable jealous rage and fired a twenty-two caliber bullet (just inches away from the top of my head and certain death) at the unsuspecting couple and missed hitting the two-timing boyfriend by a half an inch.

A full scale riot blasted throughout the auditorium a couple of hours later as my friends and I along with several thousand other terrified rock fans were dodging not only bullets from jealous girl friends, but we also were ducking frequently because of the hundreds of whiskey bottles that were being thrown at random everywhere. Bottles became guided missiles as they were flying from the balconies and finding their targets below. Police and officials frantically turned on the house lights and stopped the show but the fighting and bottle throwing increased with greater intensity. After the evening came to a climactic close, most of us incurred no injuries and walked out of the melee as rock and roll survivors.

The rock and roll shows were considered taboo as parents and clergymen alike remained opposed to them on religious and moral grounds. The bad publicity as a result of the wide scale rioting didn't help the sometimes called "Rock And Roll Circus" either.

The reason the Beatles and other "White" groups became millionaires after 1964 is because there was social pressure against caucasian teenagers attending predominately black rhythm and blues shows back in the early sixties. Parents as a rule forbid their kids or spouses to attend such shows. If these young rock and roll fans did go and see the brilliant black artists, then the history of rock might have been rewritten and Jackie Wilson would have stood taller in significance and influence than say a Mick Jagger. It is an ironic paradox that the Beatles and The Rolling Stones rate their favorite singers from mostly the rhythm and blues field since r&b got partially shut down as British Rock became more popular in the middle of late sixties.

It is unbelievable that rock and roll shows in the last twenty years have seen a marked increase in drugs and booze consumption. Drugs are now taken today to get high on with a supplemental musical diet that can appropriately be called "Drug-Rock." This is not to say that the early rock and rhythm singers didn't digest such expensive delights. If they did consume any dope, drugs, pot or whatever, they never showed it as far as their amazing stage presentations proved. In the fifties and early sixties, rock music ruled over any drugs instead of drugs taking over and ruling rock like it does today. For example, it is hard for anyone to imagine a Bobby Rydell or a Bobby Vee acting like a tanked up Mick Jagger in their respective live shows. In the height of their fame in 1960-63, both of them would have been laughed at and ridiculed for such obscene and outrageous behavior.

By attending a rock concert of today like a Summer Rock Festival, it would be like signing into an insane asylum. During a concert at Arrowhead Station in Kansas City, I had to check on a press pass in the first aid room. There was an enclosed room (with no windows) adjacent to the first aid area where security guards were putting several rock fans that had overdosed on heroin, PCP (Angel Dust), Cocaine, Black Beauties, and LSD. To witness their withdrawls for even just a few seconds, is a devastating sight to watch. They were screaming, kicking and twisting around in such a tormented and demented way that what was a basically harmless event, drugs are now making them evidently life threatening. The early concern for teenagers attending rock shows over twenty years ago has now gone from a benign situation to a malignant horror.

Many weirdos like the late Jim Morrison who pissed on stage to Screaming Jay Hawkins who would emerge from a coffin on stage with his skull called Henry have helped introduce shock and smock to rock and roll. Satanic Rock that hungers on worshipping Satan instead of God has gotten totally out of control. For example, there is a group in Wisconsin who call themselves Venom. Their advertisements solicite business for the Satan-inspired unit by a morbid invitation which reads— "Welcome to Hell."

If the aforementioned isn't enough to draw the attention of today's youth, then more drastic measures are implemented. One of rock's current heroes is Ozzy Osbourne who decided to get into the area of animal abuse by biting the heads off of bats.

. . . And if that doesn't accomplish anything in getting record deals for the mega bucks of today, then more bizarre tactics are needed for the ultimate shock wave. In England, a Punk-Rock aggregation who called themselves Antisocial, ran an advertisement that they were looking for a subject that would allow his own human head to be used as a stage prop to be placed in a guillotine for decapitation. As a financial reward, the group promised to pay the beneficiary of the deceased one-hundred thousand dollars for compensation. Incredibly, nearly five death-wishers responded to this piece of nonsense. Luckily, the British government stepped in and refused to let this barbaric plan become a reality.

Because of covert drug activity at the arena's and venues today, security has tightened to the point that current rock fans can't get ten feet near their singing idols. If anyone tries to get closer to his or her hero, he may be putting his life in danger. Look what happened at Altamont where the Hell's Angels were acting as security for the Rolling Stones and literally bludgeoned a black male patron to death with pool cues.

In another incident, a young beautiful female admirer of Bad Company's Paul Rogers in Kansas City once tried to get near him backstage when he was climbing into a long black limousine. The brunette fan was polite as she could possibly be as she veered toward Rogers. As she got close to him, Rogers threw up his right arm and rudely shoved the disillusioned girl away from him.

Over twenty years ago, ardent fans could enter the backstage areas untouched by nervous security guards and go into their hero's dressing rooms without fear of being bounced out on their ears. (In 1963, my thirteen year old sister squeezed into Jerry Butler's dressing room for an autograph whereby he asked her for a date.)

Nowadays, a reporter or a fan has to go through a lot of red tape by making some kind of arrangements with the record company who will tell that person to contact the artist's management agency and the agency will tell them to contact the local promoter who is putting on the show. The promoter will tell the perspective interviewer to contact the record company—hence, back to square one! These kind of procedures have now made backstage the loneliest place in the world to be caught dead or alive in.

There have been instances where security was as tight as a Boa Constrictor that the rock stars themselves have been kept out from entering their own performances! Carl Perkins was turned away by a security doorman from entering a surprise party held in his honor by the Beatles.

Another case in point is when Detroit rocker, Bob Seger, showed up as a surprise guest during an outdoor concert date at Kansas City's Arrowhead Stadium on July 30, 1978. Seger was going to make an unexpected appearance on the "Summer Rock II" festival that starred the evening's listed entertainers—The Eagles, Linda Rondstadt, and Dan Fogelberg with a surprise visit by Jackson Browne. The security guards at the gate didn't recognize Bob Seger and he didn't have the proper credentials required for entrance and was embarrassingly barred from entering.

Rock and roll in the eighties now still continues the legacy of being a springboard for sex, violence and revolution.

THE ROCK AND WRESTLING CONNECTION
(1958-'62)

Even professional wrestling had a mixed marriage of rock and violence, at least twenty-eight years before Cyndi Lauper and Wrestlemania made national press headlines in 1985.

The mega-bucks weren't there in the fifties as they are today, but several grapplers way back then realized the potential of exploiting rock and roll with their own field of wrestling.

For example, Ricki Starr, the ballet dancer turned pro wrestler in the late fifties, became such a popular teenage idol in the New York City area that he was eventually signed to a recording contract with RCA Victor. Ricki would use his bare feet and toes to his own great advantage by tickling and drop-kicking his opponents into submission, much to the dismay and amusement of his fans. Ricki ultimately fought many successful ring battles, but he also sang as equally as well, too.

In Saint Joseph, Missouri, the late promoter, Gus Karras, was bringing the top ranked wrestlers from around the world including such legends as Ed "Strangler" Lewis, Lou Thesz, Verne Gagne, Dick "The Bruiser" Afflis, and his biggest draw ever in the late Argentina Rocca.

One of the promoter Karrases best local favorites was a ratty-looking tough guy with a duck tail and long black sideburns. He lived up to this "rebel" image by having the nickname, Larry "Elvis" Hamilton. His ring wars in this small midwestern city was usually waged and fought against a southerner by the name of Rip

Hawk. The Saint Joseph City Auditorium was usually a sell-out when these two adversaries were matched up against each other in the ring.

Just before one of their brutal matches in 1958, Larry (Saint Joseph's answer to Elvis Presley) began singing "Hound Dog" with his acoustical flat-top guitar perched in front of him as his only form of accompaniment. In front of his screaming admirers, Larry changed the words to the aforementioned song by crooning "Chicken Hawk"—("Ya' ain't nuttin' but a Chicken Hawk, cryin' all the time—") which was directed at belittling his opponent.

While Larry was performing right in the middle of his song, Rip Hawk came charging into the ring and snuck up behind Larry, whereby the feisty blond with a flat top hair style, grabbed the guitar and smashed it into tiny pieces over Hamilton's skull. Larry went after Rip Hawk in a wild epileptic rage and chased after him all over the arena, including the balcony, hallways, and also the front auditorium lobby where Larry actually picked up and smashed a long park bench in trying to throw it at the Hawk. Surprisingly, the two of them wound up outside in the street in front of the auditorium where a bloodbath ensued. This wrestling show became reality that night, as both grapplers had to be detained by the police, the promoter, and some of the other wrestlers.

Larry "Elvis" Hamilton was standing up for what Elvis and rock and roll stood for, and the licking he took that fateful unforgettable wintery night for what he believed in was all-inspiring. Hamilton took one hell of a beating—and baby, that was all for Elvis and rock and roll.

Harley Race, a known twister by the town's oldster's, lived in a small town—Savannah, Missouri, back in 1963.

During one summer evening while living in a small cabin adjacent to a filling station, Harley was abruptly awoken by the Rocktones, an instrumental band that played original numbers as well as selections originated by the Ventures. The two musicians—guitarist Carrol Howard and drummer Bob Kinder (yours truly) were jamming outside of this Airway Station at eleven o'clock at night when Harley came running out of his cabin with no shirt on and went directly to the station's night attendant and told him that he was going to smash the drums over my head, if the music didn't stop immediately, if not sooner.

TWO TALL GAL MAT STARS WITH NO PEER!

Seated . . .
5' 9", 140
Lorraine
Johnson

Standing . . .
5' 9", 145
Penny
Banner

Actually, throughout the years, many wrestlers recorded musical and also comedy records. Several burley scrappers with an equally brutal singing voice to match, tried to become pop vocalists. The list of grappling warblers is a long one which includes beefy performers as the Crusher, Fred Blassie, Argentina Rocca, etc., but none of them have clicked with any chart hits.

Thus, rock and wrestling did flirt with each other over two decades ago before the marriage of rock and wrestling were finally realized by rock star, Cyndi Lauper, World Wrestling Federation Champion—Hulk Hogan, Wendi Williams (the female champion who is managed by Miss Lauper) and the twenty-four hour music channels in MTV and VHI.

RUDY LEWIS AND THE DRIFTERS

The Drifters started in the music field at New York City, back in 1953, by leading and pioneering the way for many other rhythm and blues groups by contributing with their own unique style. This Gotham unit always possessed that extra "Uumph" in what they utilized in all their arrangements, that have helped make them extraordinary to view in person at a rock and roll show.

The Drifters was actually formed in the latter part of '53, when the late and great, Clyde McPhatter helped start the group and became their very first lead singer. Their first record of "Money Honey" for Atlantic Records was a tremendous seller, proving that they had that special magic from the beginning. It did not take any time at all for the Drifters to become the number one rhythm and blues vocal group of the nation.

When Clyde McPhatter got enlisted into the Army in 1955, the remaining Drifters continued to record for Atlantic and continually appeared in many theatres around the fifty states.

Their very first record without McPhatter that ultimately became a two-sided hit for them was "Adorable" and "Steamboat." These songs were soon followed with yet another double-sided chart winners in "Ruby Baby" and "Your Promise To Be Mine." It is a well known fact that all four of the aforementioned sides came out of one historical session in Hollywood, which was supervised by the legendary Atlantic producer, Nesuhi Ertegun.

The lead tenor of Johnny Moore took over as the lead voice of the Drifters through the middle to late fifties.

The Drifters restructured themselves in late 1958, when a group known as the Crowns, with lead singer,

63

Ben E. King, became "The (new) Drifters" under the guidance of George Treadwell. Their 1959 release, "There Goes My Baby," was the first rock and roll ballad record that actually featured a full orchestra of strings for the background.

The Drifters has always been a favorite concert draw. They have broken attendance-records at such mecca's as the Apollo Theatre in New York City and the Howard Theatre in Washington, D.C. The group's appearance in "The Biggest Show of Stars of 1957-58" boosted their already growing legion of fans nationwide. In 1959, they were a part of the fabulous "Dick Clark Caravan of Stars" that was touring from coast to coast which also showcased the impeccable talents of LaVern Baker, Lloyd Price, Annette, the Skyliners, and Paul Anka.

During 1961, the Drifter's lineup included Charley Thomas, lead singer; Doc Green, baritone; Rudy Lewis, tenor: Elsberry Hobbs, bass; and Bill Davis on the guitar who accompanied the group.

It was during 1961 that Rudy Lewis replaced Ben E. King as the lead singer of the unit.

Supersonic Attractions presented "The Show of Stars" in 1963 that starred such luminaries as Jerry Butler, the Impressions, Major Lance, Bob and Earl, Gorgeous George, Sam and Dave, and the one and only Drifters.

It was during this gigantic show's stopover in Kansas City that many young, excited rock and rollin' white kids had the pleasure and the privilege to see many of rock's biggest acts of the day.

However, during the second half of the show, a riot ensued as bottles were being thrown, bullets were being shot out of hand pistols and many people panicked and started heading for the exits and lobbyways of the auditorium.

After the melee started, Rudy Lewis was seen running through the east lobby of the Kansas City Auditorium. Looking both bewildered and excited, Rudy could not understand what had happened and why people were getting so crazy and out of hand. He expressed disbelief and disgust that such behavior on the part of some of the rowdies and drunken patrons had stopped and interrupted this night's concert. Rudy was very pleasant to get to know and visit with. He mentioned how excited he was about the Drifters' new and upcoming release for Atlantic and he expressed a keen interest and desire to play the Midwest audiences more often as they seemed to be "Very responsive and loyal to our group (The Drifters) and to all of the songs that we do perform for them on stage." Rudy also mentioned that his favorite song at the time was "Vaya Con Dios" and that he enjoyed doing some songs in a "Spanish-style of presentation." "I like to feature a lot of variety to my singing and my voice," said Lewis enthusiastically. "I am so glad that George (Treadwell) and the Drifter's organization has given me the honor and the privilege of singing with them. But, also, I am looking forward to a solo singing career that is similar to what Ben E. King has done in his own successful career. I feel our music is tailored for everybody. We can do romantic ballads and we can also really get with it on fast numbers."

Rudy's rich distinctively infectious tonality makes his voice the most recognizable of all the Drifter's biggest early sixties hits. His lead vocals on "Up On The Roof," "On Broadway," "Some Kind of Wonderful" and many others led Atlantic Records to record Rudy on some solo recording ventures.

Unfortunately, Rudy Lewis passed away in 1963, which had left a big void in the Drifters that was felt for many years afterward.

REQUIEM OF A LEGENDARY RECORD PRODUCER
ROBERT "BUMPS" BLACKWELL

September 14, 1955, has been called a crucial testing period in the history of popular music. It was on this very date that Little Richard cut "Tutti Frutti" at Cosimo Matussa's J&M Studios. Richard was backed by the Crescent City Rhythm Section with Art Rupe hiring "Bumps" Blackwell to engineer and produce the session for the "Georgia Peach." It has been well established that "Tutti Frutti" helped mark the beginning of the rock and roll explosion.

Robert "Bumps" Blackwell is a legend in his own time. Blackwell, along with a handful of other musical geniuses from the early fifties including Sam Phillips, helped mold what later became an explosion that sent shock waves around the world that are still being felt today. "Bumps" Blackwell is a man of great vision — a brilliant man that discovered and produced such legendary talents as Lou Rawls, Sam Cooke, Redbone, and the aforementioned Little Richard. Blackwell is a man of many qualities that are very unique in nature. He is a record producer, songwriter, arranger, music director, orchestra leader, promoter, and record entrepreneur.

It was back in 1955 that Blackwell launched the careers of many other artists and helped discover and launch the careers of Lloyd Price, Larry Williams, Lee Allen, and Don and Dewey, just to name a few.

Blackwell also discovered the seventies rock band, Redbone, and took them into the studio from an Indian reservation out West. In the early seventies, "Come and

Get Your Love" was recorded by this native American group for Epic Records and became one of the biggest songs of that early decade.

"Bumps" Blackwell is a man of many contrasts but is highly opinionated about this business of music. He is both bitter but still holds a certain amount of enthusiasm about the music industry today. His mild mannerisms along with his candid remarks concerning today's sometimes stale music scene makes him somewhat baffling. "This singer called Boy George is a mere imitation of Sam Cooke," exclaims Blackwell. "I often see many people making it in the business today that is a copy of what I have learned and instilled in many of my students which comes right back to me. For example, you will have a student of a student of a student that eventually evolves back to me and many of the people I have worked with. When you see Boy George and listen to him, you'll be hearing the influence of Sam Cooke upon the student, Boy George, and Sam Cooke I taught also."

There are many disciples and students of Little Richard around today in John Fogerty, Bob Segar, Eric Clapton, Paul McCartney and even Van Halen. Blackwell, however, believes that the musical menu today is lacking in a lot of important nutrients. "I feel that music today is digressing—much of today's music scene seems to be out of time, out of step and the music today is lacking versatility and showmanship. It seems to me that many of the acts and producers today are prostituting themselves. You've got to be a shoe salesman for one thing to get in the business and even a drug addict— dope peddlers in order to get in today's music business."

"Bumps" has been blinded by the eye disease of glaucoma but this doesn't deter him from engaging in fruitful projects. His ambitious tenacity is very much instilled in him. "I just had to get back into the music business to do my thing," he explains. "You have to get into the system to get anything out of the system," he realistically admits. "I want to start having some of the old format of packaged shows once again—in other words, bring showmanship back into the mainstream arena of popular music. So, I am concentrating on some live concert ideas for the future. I am also getting back into producing and become an artist myself."

Because of Blackwell's Indian heritage, he wants to work closely in producing many promising Indian artists like his current group, Night Wind. Blackwell is busy producing an up-and-coming new country music contemporary vocalist named Marilyn Murphy.

Blackwell, who still makes his home in Los Angeles, hinted that Little Richard is working on a "soul-stirring" project with contemporary overtones that will not be satanic at all in nature. Blackwell relates that Little Richard has been preaching and performing the Gospel on several records and also has been putting his talents to great use by preaching on good against evil in the L.A. area.

"Bumps" Blackwell is indeed one of our finest pioneering producer-promoters in the early history of popular music.

TEEN IDOLS AND ROCK AND ROLL SCREAMERS
(1959-'63)

After Elvis Presley revolutionized popular music, a new breed of singers began springing up and taking a piece of the rock and roll action.

By 1959, the floodgates opened with some fresh new faces in rockdom. These hopefuls had visions of future stardom as they traveled to many of the top music venues around the country. Many of them sang rock-a-ballads, a musical trend that combined love ballads with a light or heavy four-four rock beat. From Philadelphia came the likes of Frankie Avalon with "Gingerbread," "Why," and "Venus," followed by Philly-based Chancellor Records labelmate, Fabian with "I'm a Man," "Turn Me Loose," "Hound Dog Man," and "Tiger." Bobby Rydell is another Philly entry who was on the charts in 1959 with "Swingin' School" and later clicked with "Sway," "Forget Him," and the great swing-ballad in "Volare." Bobby even jumped on the dance craze bandwagon when he came up with an early sixties dance tune called "The Fish." Bobby recorded for Cameo Records out of Philadelphia along with Chubby Checker who clicked in 1959 with a novelty Chipmunk styling called "The Class." His biggest claim to fame was the dance fad that revolutionized this art form with "The Twist," the first real floor stomper that separated couples for the first time from doing the popular Jitterbug.

Paul Anka came down from Toronto to become a major headliner of rock and roll with his 1959 ballads of "Puppy Love," "My Home Town," and "Lonely Boy." Paul's previous hit that launched him into stardom was the 1957 release on ABC Paramount in "Diana," a ballad he wrote for his ex-babysitter.

Pat Boone was still clicking in the latter fifties through 1963 with "April Love," Little Richard's "Tutti Frutti" and "Speedy Gonzalos." In helping to secure his own future after the hits stopped, Pat joined the AmWay Company and was awarded the gold pin for sales excellence. Pat, along with his wife Shirley, also have a variety talk show on the CBN (Christian Broadcasting Network) channel.

Bobby Vee achieved a long string of chart winners after being discovered in Fargo, North Dakota after filling in at a dance in Moorehead, Minnesota, for Buddy Holly in February of 1959, as a result of Holly's Iowa plane tragedy.

There were other teen idols that covered the pop market like a blanket between 1959 until the British-Beatles invasion of January, 1964. Carl Dopkins, Junior came out of Cincinnati, Ohio with a couple of medium-paced ballads that gave him some notoriety in "My Heart Is An Open Book" and "Lucky Devil."

Johnny Restivo was a young sixteen year-old who had won a body building contest that set the charts on fire with a song that was his own personal theme and also the very first talent that dealt with a particular condition of a rock singer in "The Shape I'm In" for RCA-Victor.

Jesse Lee Turner kept novelty-rock music alive in 1959 with "Little Space Girl" and followed it with "I'm the Little Space Girl's Father." Dick Caruso was a distant relative of the famed opera star, Enrico Caruso. His dark handsome good looks was favoring him to become another popular teen swooner. Unfortunately, after co-starring on rock shows with Jimmy Clanton in 1959, his subsequent recordings for MGM Records didn't put a very big niche on the charts. Jack Scott was a premier rockabilly-teen ballad star who dented the top forty with "My True Story," "Geraldine," "Goodbye Baby (Bye Bye)," "Bella," "What In the World's Come Over You," and "Burning Bridges," in the late fifties through the early part of the next decade. Johnny Burnette sang Rockabilly with his brother Dorsey and Paul Burlison in the Johnny Burnette Trio. He had won a spot on Ted Mack's Amateur Hour and also made a movie, "Rock, Rock, Rock" with Alan Freed, Chuck Berry and Frankie Lymon and the Teenagers. After the Johnny Burnette Trio cut a brilliant classic LP in 1957 for Coral Records, he pursued a successful solo career as a teen idol in the early sixties with "You're Sixteen," "Dreamin'," and may others while brother Dorsey got lucky with "Tall Oak Tree" (Both Johnny and Dorsey wrote hits like "Waitin' In School" and "Stood Up" for Ricky Nelson). In 1979, just prior to his heart attack which killed him, Dorsey won the Country Music Association award as the Best New Country Vocalist of the year. This is an irony for Dorsey to win such an award since he has been in the music business since 1957, over twelve years before Nashville finally recognized him as a viable artist to deal with. Another teen idol who got his start during the 1959 period is Johnny Tillotson. Originally a hillbilly singer, Johnny made it on the rock and roll circuit by crooning country ballads in a pop fashion like "Talk Back Trembling Lips" and "Send Me the Pillow You Dream On." He also achieved some brief notice from the teen magazines when Johnny had two more hits in the early sixties with "Poetry In Motion" and "Dreamy Eyes."

There were many others that became teen favorites including Frankie Sardo who was on tour with Buddy Holly and appeared with Buddy at his last concert in Clear Lake, Iowa. Frankie's only memorable disc was "Classroom" backed with "Fake Out" for ABC Paramount in 1959. Dion (with the Belmonts) also appeared at the historic Clear Lake concert. This Bronx native enjoyed considerable fame with his group on the Laurie label out of New York. Their biggest hits are among rock's finest classics in "I Wonder Why," "Where or When," and "A Teenager In Love." Dion (whose lase name is Dimucci) went solo in 1960 when he began a long string of top forty hits with "Runaround Sue," "The Wanderer," "Lonely Teenager," "Sandy," "I Was Born To Cry," "Little Diane," among others for Laurie. His last hits were for Columbia when he had three monster recordings in "Ruby Baby" in 1963 and "Donna the Prima Donna," along with "Drip Drop" in 1963. Dion was actually the top teen idol that was very much affected by the Beatles in 1964. After the British invaded these shores, Dion wasn't heard from again until he had one more triumphant recording with his old label, Laurie, that made a somber social statement that raised our consciousness with "Abraham, Martin and John" in 1968. Based out of Miami, Florida, Dion now sings gospel songs served up for the Lord and appears at gospel concerts as well as the Seven Hundred Club on CBN.

Floyd Robinson was a brief artist with RCA in 1959 when his country-styled ballad, "Making Love" put him temporarily into the rock and roll big leagues. Some of the other one-shot artists include Frank Ifield ("I remember You"), Larry Hall ("Sandy"), Sanford Clark ("The Fool"), Bobby Pedrick, Junior ("White Bucks & Saddle Shoes"—he later had hits in the late seventies under his real name of Robert John), Scott Engel ("The Livin' End"), Don French ("Lonely Saturday Night"), Dante, Johnny Angel, and Tony Bellus from Philadelphia with his NRC swing-ballad of "Robbin' The Cradle." Bob McPhadden and a crazy character called Dor on record topped the charts in 1959 with a novelty song, "The Mummy" ("I want my Mummy"—remember?). Bob Mc-Phadden and Dor was actually singer-poet, Rod McKuen.

Many other aspiring singers from the days of 1959 that had more than one hit include Buzz Clifford ("Baby Sittin' Boogie" and "Forever"), Paul Evans ("Midnite Special," "Happy-Go-Lucky-Me," and "Seven Little Girls Sitting In The Back Seat"), Bobby "Boris" Pickett ("Monster Mash," and "Monsters' Holiday"), Gene Pitney, Ray Peterson ("Tell Laura I Love Her," "Corinna, Corinna"), Buddy Knox, Jimmy Bowen, and Mark Dinning.

Mark Dinning had one of the most popular "Death" recordings in 1959. In an interview, he explained how the song was created—"Jean Surrey who is my sister wrote it while she was still living in Dinners Grove, Illinois. We recorded 'Teen Angel' in October, 1959, at Owen Bradley's studios in Nashville. My sister had a teenage daughter that took (teen) magazines and stuff, and she was reading a disc jockey magazine talking about kids, and she read an article about a disc jockey and he was talking about kids you know, throughout the country, and he said—'I hear all the people putting down the teenagers of today and how rough and tumble they are like undisciplined; and they're all a bunch of little devils. From my own experience, I happen to know quite a few teen angels,' and, that's where she got her idea."

"In England they banned it because they considered it "Too bloody awful," admitted Mark with a grin.

Bobby Comstock from New York was among the first (if not actually the first) to play all of the instruments of a single recording. After he achieved two extra solo hits in "Tennessee Waltz" and "Jambalya," Bobby played all of the instruments in the studio on Freddie Cannon's 1963 rocker, "Patty Baby." Bobby and his group, the Counts in '63 had another major hit in "Let's Stomp." Bobby and his group backs up most of the stars that is featured on all of Richard Nader's "Doo-Wopp At The Garden" concerts at Madison Square Garden's Felt Forum in New York City.

Gerry Granahan had a similar career in the late fifties to that of Buddy Holly. He not only achieved hits as a soloist in "No Chemise, Please" and "Girl Of My Dreams" for Sunbeam, but also simultaneously garnered several successful platters with his group, Dickey Do and the Don'ts with "Click Clack" and "Nee Nee Na Na Na Na Nu Nu" for the Swan Label. (Holly had a solo career while also putting out songs on vinyl with his group, the Crickets.)

Many other "Teen Idols" between 1959 and 1963 that deserve honorable mention are Larry Finnegan ("Dear One"), Tony Allen ("Night Owl"), Don and Dewey, Bobby Curtola ("Fortuneteller"), Crash Craddock ("Don't Destroy Me"), Brian Hyland, Jimmy Jones ("Good Timin' " and "Handy Man"), Bob Jaxon came out with "Beach

Party" even before surf and beach movies were made, and Johnny Ferguson sang a sentimental love-ballad about a girl named "Angela Jones."

Rod Bernard from Louisiana churned his soaring—pleading ballad of "This Should Go On Forever" for Argo Records with his group, the Twisters. He also cut numerous sides on the Jin label out of Shreveport including a song called "Colinda."

Faron Young, Ferlin Husky, Jim Reeves, and Sheb Wooley all crossed over from the country field into pop with their hits in the late fifties and early sixties. Husky and Wooley also doubled on their respective recordings as a comedy character that would cut parodies of hits of the day. Husky's favorite character was Simon Crum while Sheb spoofed many hits in the disguise of his crazy man—Ben Colder. Colder would parody such recordings as "Still" (—"I wish I had a Still—") and "Harper Valley PTA" (PTA stood for "Party Time Already" in his version of Jeannie C. Riley's song).

Warren Smith from the Sun Records stable and country-billy crooner, George Jones toured on the Grand Old Opry tours in 1962 together with Carl Perkins and headliner, Johnny Cash.

Warren Smith sang his Liberty sides like "I Don't Believe I'll Fall In Love Today" on the tour while also punching out his Sun rockabilly sides with "Miss Froggie" and "Rock and Roll Ruby."

George Jones known also fondly as "the Possum," sang such classics as "The Window Up Above" and "White Lightning," the latter number being the most popular rocker of George's career that was actually written by the late Big Bopper—J. P. Richardson.

In 1959, Ronnie Hawkins and the Hawks recorded for Roulette Records in New York some of the best rock and roll ever released. Ronnie became a Johnny Come Lately rock and roll pioneer in '59 with two fast hits in his self-penned "Mary Lou" and a newer re-made arrangement of Chuck Berry's "Thirty Days" which Ronnie and the boys tagged "Forty Days." His dynamic high energy stage presentations made him a hot teen rave that should have received more publicity than he actually did back in 1959-63.

In the early sixties, Ronnie and the Hawks cut what some musicologists have believed to be the most exciting rock recording of all time in Bo Diddley's "Who Do You Love." Robbie Robertson's soaring guitar licks along with Ronnie's screaming rebel yells took this song to new heights.

While Ronnie stayed stationed in Canada, Robbie, along with drummer Levon Helm, and the rest of the Hawks eventually came to the states where they became known as the Band and eventually joined up with Bob Dylan. Robbie also co-starred in the movie, "Carney" with Jodie Foster and Gary Busey.

Ronnie Hawkins has the distinction of being the only rock pioneer from the late fifties to participate in the 1985 Band Aid African relief effort program. Ronnie joined other Canadian rock stars for their own version of a song that was similar to "We Are The World." Hawkins joined Bryan Adams, Anne Murray, Burton Cummings, and other Canadians for their own musical video contribution to the African hunger relief drive that was also musically done by the top rock stars of England and Los Angeles.

Gary Stites recorded for Carlton and his recording in 1959, "Lonely For You" was a chart number that gave him the opportunity to tour with the best rock stars of the day including the Bell Notes, Santo and Johnny, Dick Caruso, the Duprees and Jimmy Clanton. This entire aforementioned entourage toured the Midwest in

1959. Gary appeared at the Electric Theatre in Saint Joseph, Missouri and thrilled the audience with his flashy showmanship that included running from any part of the seats and aisles onto the stage at the beginning of his set. Gary would include in his gruelling routine a whole series of wild dancing along with splits, jumps and springs. He would warm up the teens in the theatre with some of the finest versions of rock and roll ever heard in doing his own arrangements of "Long Tall Sally," "Gloria Lee," "Lawdy Miss Clawdy," and then knelt down on bended knee and sang his ballad, "Lonely For You" and another love theme, "Starry Eyed" for his mid-western fans. Gary would often dress up in a casual but dressy beige-colored knit sweater with dark tight-fitting slacks and white Buck shoes, which was the chic dress in '59. Gary would constantly move on stage and touch his female fans with a romantic clasp and kiss them before venturing on into another number like "Stagger Lee." Unfortunately, his rising stardom in popular music burst by 1962 causing Gary to move back to his home state of Colorado and work at Stite's Service Station near Golden.

Another group that was on tour with Gary and Jimmy Clanton who also became teen idols as a unit in 1959 was the Bell Notes. Their hit for Time Records was the sing along novel release, "I've Had It."

There were a couple of minor teen idols that came out of Gene Vincent's Blue Caps to make some solo recordings. Both Paul Peek and Tommy Facenda hit the charts in 1959. Peek clicked with "Mother-In-Law, She's a Moocher" for Fairlane while Tommy had the big hit, "High School USA" for Atlantic. Tommy cut the song several times and included several different school district regions in Virginia, Kansas City-Saint Louis, etc. each time he recorded the rocker.

In the Fall of 1971, a rock revival show hit the Capri Theatre in Kansas City. The lineup of the show included Johnny Thunder, the Belmonts, and rock pioneer, Chuck Berry.

With less than fifty people in attendance, Chuck came on last to a scattered subdued applause. His thrown together backup band was having trouble keeping up with his repertoire and one musician in the crowd got so frustrated by what he perceived as the drummer's dragging tempo's that he jumped up and went back behind the stage to visually instruct Chuck's drummer to come alive more.

Chuck romped through his classics like "Little Quennie" and also promoted "My Ding-A-Ling" for the small throng of fans.

Chuck was obviously upset by the lack of attendance. After the concert, Berry wouldn't utter a word to nobody and refused to sign autographs.

In 1973, Chuck Berry made a return visit to Kansas City, but he played the Memorial Hall which is on the Kansas side of the mighty Mizzou. He was over two hours late for his performance but the patient audience waited for his triumphant arrival on the strength of Chuck's two Chess recordings that hit the charts in 1972 in "My Ding-A-Ling" and "Reelin' and Rockin'."

In the last eight years, Berry has lacked the fire and power in his famous stage act. He now just seems to go through the motions while performing as if the many years of wear and tear from traveling and from being jailed have now caught up with him. Chuck did tell fellow rock artist Bobby Comstock in New York that "You don't get paid for the playing but for the traveling."

When Chuck once appeared on Tom Snyder's "Tomorrow" program on NBC, he actually hit several wrong notes on the guitar that were noticeable from coast to coast. He was playing some duets with his daughter on the Snyder show when the miscues occurred.

Chuck's appearance in the 1984 Grammy Awards Show has helped keep his name from disappearing from the public eye.

While Chuck Berry could be tagged as the unheralded Crown Prince of Rock and Roll for his crisp punctuated guitar riffs and poetically imaginative lyrics that helped define rock and roll back in the fifties, Elvis Presley was being crowned as the King of Rock.

While his rockabilly and rhythm and blues counterparts kept music alive in the late forties and early fifties, it was Elvis that commercialized it before an ever growing white public following.

Elvis was influenced greatly by such diverse artists as the bluesman, Arthur "Big Boy" Crudup to Hank Snow and bluegrass man, Bill Monroe.

It is also interesting to note that in the early sixties, Elvis had several favorite songs for different reasons. He liked "Linda Lou" but would have re-named the song after one of his favorite girlfriends—"Anita Wood."

Elvis loved country music and that is why he recorded "Blue Moon of Kentucky" as his first recording for Sun.

According to El's other musical tastes, a person would never cross him by saying that you "hate" a song. He may say personally that he doesn't like a record for some reason or other, but it's not always the music he doesn't like. He loved all musical styles and also understood and respected their special meanings.

Some of Presley's favorite songs included Roy Orbison's "Running Scared," a song that Elvis would play over and over again and eventually would wear out. He also enjoyed "Great Shakin' Fever" by Dorsey Burnette and "I'll Be There" by Bobby Darin. He also included on his juke box in Graceland Mansion such songs as "Runaway" by Del Shannon and "The Girl of My Best Friend" by his soundalike imitator, Ral Donner.

There was an amusing incident that happened to Elvis while filming "Blue Hawaii." While he was singing "Hawaiian Sweetheart" on the set, Elvis was picking on his ukulele very hard. He played it so hard that in fact he literally broke it in two.

Throughout his recording career, Elvis Presley cut some of his favorite songs that helped enhance his identity as the total performer. Elvis enjoyed singing Chuck Berry's "The Promised Land" and Jimmy Reed's "Big Boss Man." Elvis would open his concerts with the 1958 Chuck Willis hit, "See See Rider." Unlike the Beatles who wrote many of their own numbers, Elvis borrowed heavily from New York's Tin Pan Ally composers including Jerry Leiber, Mike Stoller and Otis Blackwell. It was obvious that his strong points were his strong tenor singing voice, along with a macho working man-blue collar image he had projected to the public since 1955. Elvis Presley's charisma as a hero to the middle and lower class has even continued long after his untimely death from a heart attack or a possible accidental drug overdose that unfortunately occurred on August 17, 1977, at his Graceland home in Memphis.

Bo Diddley (real name, Elias McDaniel after becoming adopted) has what is considered to be "The Baddest —Sassiest Guitar in Rock History." This bawdy-acting overweight bluesman from McComb, Mississippi, via Chicago, got started while working in the chitlin circuit at such clubs as the 708 Club. Bo Diddley was once a boxer who like Jackie Wilson and James Brown turned to music as a longer lasting profession instead.

At the age of seventeen, Bo signed a record pact with Leonard Chess at Chess Records after claiming that "Everybody else slammed the doors in my face." Bo's first record was "Bo Diddley," the first song named after the artist himself. The record showcased the Bo Diddley Beat, otherwise known as "The Tradesman's Knock." This infectious beat has its origins in Africa but Bo utilized it into a commercial sound.

After "Bo Diddley" was released, all the record hops around the country featured the Bo Diddley beat. Other artists utilized this rhythm pattern into their songs like the Rolling Stones and Buddy Holly's "Not Fade Away," Duane Eddy put it in "Cannonball" and Dee Clark used it to great advantage in "Hey Little Girl."

Many of Bo Diddley's early records and club-concert dates were enhanced by his marraccas man, Jerome and also his half-sister, the Duchess. Bo's wiggle that includes his legs gyrating back and forth was picked up by Elvis in 1956 when the King visited Bo's show at New York's Apollo Theatre.

In 1959, Bo made a novelty recording, "Say Man" that gave him a hit which was followed by "Say Man, Back Again." The song was a spontaneous ad lib that found Bo and a friend spewing out jive talk and insults at each other about "ugly" wives and girlfriends. Bo also clicked with "You Can't Judge a Book By It's Cover."

Bo Diddley broke touring stage record in October, 1961 at Kansas City's Municipal Auditorium when he appeared a grand total of four times with each of the four sets being over a half-hour in duration. No other concert artist in the history of the popular music actually has appeared in four different sets in one single evening's time on a packaged show with several record stars on the same bill. The reason this occurred is because the evening's headliners, Jackie Wilson and Jerry Lee Lewis didn't show up that unforgettable night.

Bo was dressed for the occasion that wild night by fixing himself all up in a white shirt, black bow tie and red and black checkered suit coat. Many of the paying patrons did get tired of Bo, Jerome and the Duchess and started yelling after Bo's fourth set by hollering such tirad's at him such as "We've heard enough" or "Bo Diddley go home!" The Bo Diddley Trio stood up to a lot of criticism by playing their hearts out to the five thousand plus rock and roll fans. Bo even predated the Psychedelic era by demonstrating that night some wild feedback on his Gretch guitar by sliding the pick all over the bass strings and making them electronically sound like a jet plane taking off and thunderously crashing. Bo's funny shaped rectangular axe made him among the very first premier guitarists to deviate from conventional and more traditional guitar body designs by using a uniquely, custom designed six-string model.

Bo Diddley cut numerous albums tailored for the musical trends of the day. Some of his theme oriented LP's included "Bo Diddley's A Lover," "Bo Diddley's A Twister," "Bo Diddley's Beach Party," "Bo Diddley Goes Surfing" and "Bo Diddley's A Gunslinger." There were many other interesting long plays including "Two Great Guitars" with Chess Stablemate, Chuck Berry The "Gunslinger" album was made as a result of the many popular television westerns as well as recordings that were popular as a result of the western themes like Marty Robbin's classic of "El Paso" and Duane Eddy's "Ring Of Fire."

Bo Diddley stole the show from Jerry Lee Lewis, Frankie Valli, Duane Eddy, etc. at Richard Nader's Rock and Roll Revival Spectacular at New York's Madison Square Garden on June 11, 1971. Bo literally made love to his guitar that evening by performing an orgasmic kind of ritual and sensually played with it on the floor while still stroking his axe like he would a beautiful woman while all this time still licking his chops off his strings like batting bricks off a building. Bo's brimming over with his accented blues runs brought hundreds of people into the aisles with "I'm A Man."

One of the biggest crowds he ever appeared in front of in his entire career occurred on July 6, 1985 at the Liberty Memorial in Kansas City when he shook up the predominately young under thirty outdoor concert crowd (mostly twenty to thirty years his junior) with his crazy gyrations. Bo headlined this record breaking Kansas City Spirit Fest concert that was sponsored by oldies station WHB. The WHB Oldies Party set an all time drawing record by drawing over three hundred and fifty thousand people—the largest crowd for any single event in Kansas City history.

Bo was brilliant that evening as he thrilled the over-sized throng to some of his better blues drippings in "I'm A Man" and "Who Do You Love." Bo was angered at times because a man was video taping his set from the front of the stage whereby Bo asked him to remove his video equipment—"I don't remember talking to you," screamed Bo. He also waved off a photographer from the backstage area and also complained of the spotlight man having the stage lights shining too brightly on him—"It feels like two freight trains blinding you by coming at each side of you at the same time—turn that sonofabitch off!"

In spite of his bitching, complaining and feisty attitude that singular night, Diddley came out of his set smelling like roses.

Bo does revere his fans though. He admitted to me in August, 1981, that as long as the people come out, I'll still keep on entertaining them."

After seeing him perform in person, anyone can understand that there is only one Bo Diddley around and rock and roll has a lot to thank Bo for in his enormous contributions to the music scene during the last thirty years.

Fats Domino was the all-time leading chart leader in fusing rhythm and blues and pop together into a finished sellable product that knows no boundaries. Dave Bartholomew and Fats Domino together wrote a string of hits that garnered the Fatman from New Orleans a grand total of over twenty-three gold singles. His recording career was so successful that by 1963, Fats had surpassed over fifty million recordings which at that time made him only one out of five artists to garner such an achievement (only Elvis Presley, Bing Crosby, Frank Sinatra and Judy Garland along with Mr. Domino had reached and surpassed the coveted fifty million mark in sales).

Fats never did achieve the status of having a number one hit single in spite of his many other accomplishments including appearances in movies from the fifties in "Do Re Mi," "The Big Beat," Disc Jockey Jamboree," and "The Girl Can't Help It." He had more charted hits than anybody else except Elvis by the year 1964 but none of them got any higher than number four which was accomplished by the blues-rock ballad, "Blueberry Hill" in 1956.

Mr. Domino's style of performing in front of cameras and audiences bordered on simplicity and was very benign by today's own standards set by the artists of the eighties. Fats was thoroughly effective by jabbing short strokes at the piano while his shoulders would quiver and twist around. After a quick solo run, Fats would act like he'd got a case of heebie jeebies by twisting and turning his upper torso and look at the crowd with a brief smile and then quickly look away and play a few more strains.

During a performance in England back in the mid-sixties, Fats would turn his fans on by getting up from the piano stool, by standing erect and began pushing his heavy baby grand piano across the stage while playing all the runs without ever losing a beat.

Fats, who likes to wear perfume before going on stage, headlined Alan Freed's Rock and Roll Show at the Brooklyn Paramount in 1957 and the gross from his appearance there was an unprecedented two-hundred and twenty thousand dollars at the time.

Fats also starred in "The Biggest Show of Stars For 1961" and returned the following year and co-headlined with cronner Brook Benton in "The Biggest Show of Stars For 1962—Spring Edition." This was an historic concert tour from the standpoint that neither one of them had ever toured together before.

Fats also at one time gave another fifties legend, Little Richard, a playing job.

As opposed to other American 1950's rock stars like Gene Vincent and Jerry Lee Lewis, Fats Domino did not tour England until 1967 during the main thrust of the British Invasion which in turn started creating a hybrid product, Psychedelia, during the late sixties. The Beatle's manager, Brian Epstein was able to secure the Saville Theatre in London's Shaftesbury Avenue during Easter week of 1967 where he headlined Fats Domino and his Orchestra.

The lineup at the Saville that particular week was unreal. Gerry and the Pacemakers and the Bee Gees opened the concert for Fats! In spite of this interesting lineup, the Saville Theatre did not sell out for one night! (Fats eventually achieved superstar status in Britain just a few years later.)

Jerry Lee Lewis is anything but boring. So many stories and volumes of magazine articles and books have been written about this Ferriday, Louisiana Fireball that originally brought the rock and roll world to its knees in 1957 with "Whole Lotta Shakin' Goin' On," "Great Balls Of Fire," "Breathless" and "High School Confidential" for Sun Records. These songs were so popular that many rock and roll writers speculated that in just a short time, Jerry Lee would replace Elvis as the "King Of Rock and Roll." The Charlton Publication, "Songs and Stars" for August, 1958, came out with a full blown picture cover and article spread that reported the following—"He's becoming the nation's number one teenage idol." Radio station WHB in Kansas City reported on their "Sound Off" program popularity poll that Jerry Lee Lewis was leading Elvis by a wide margin of two to one in deciding who deserves to be tagged the "King." Maybe the poll was a bit biased since Jerry Lee was appearing at the Kansas City Auditorium as the headliner for "The Biggest Show of Stars for 1958." Many callers that voted for Jerry Lee probably had attended the concert and was convincingly impressed with his gyrations that included shaking orgasms with piano stools being kicked clear across the stage floor and vibrating contortions from Lewis that deservingly gave him publicity as "The Great Ball of Fire," "The Blond Liberace," and "The Untamed Rock and Roll Fury."

Jerry Lee has felt that he is the best artist in popular music. His ego balloons whenever other famous rockers are mentioned to him as being fans of his including Elton John, Ringo Starr and Tom Jones who have taken Jerry Lee's style and turned it into their own vehicle. An accomplished pianist himself, Elton John has admittedly been influenced by him—"Nobody's taking my style," cries Jerry Lee. "I don't think Elton John is taking my style. Whenever people look at him (Elton John), they think of the old master. All he is doing is promoting Jerry Lee Lewis in a complementary way."

"Fifty years from now, Jerry Lee Lewis will be like Hank Williams, Jimmie Rodgers, and Al Jolson. I'm a stylist not a Johnny come lately. I am what I am. I set the trend and they follow."

Jerry Lee was the first fifties rocker to have long hair that actually reached well below his chin. He was a rebel with or without a cause—it really didn't matter 'cause Jerry Lee is just going through life being Jerry Lee. He certainly was an original one of a kind rock pioneer to do unorthodox antics that gave him free press and strongly opinionated public attention. You either love or hate him—there is simply no in between. Jerry Lee is proud to be tagged "The Pied Piper of Rock." "I am the original Hippie," roars Jerry Lee. "You might consider me a revolutionary. I've done and tried it all but I have never changed my style."

Jerry Lee has had problems from time to time with fellow artists as well as fans. While he was on an Australian tour bill in 1959, Jerry Lee was the third from last in the lineup—only Tommy Sands and Paul Anka came on and headlined the shows after him. Jerry Lee felt that he should close the shows instead of Sands and Anka. In most of the Australian stops, he did manage to "Steal" the show away from a more tamer and benign Paul Anka and the rest of the stars on the touring bill. Jerry Lee not only reported this fact back in the United States, but Jack Scott and Freddie Cannon reported the same information to Jerry Lee's fan club president, Kay Martin. (Johnny and the Hurricanes and Mark Dinning were also part of the '59 Australian rock and roll tour.) There was some criticism leveled at Jerry

Lee as a result of the Australian experience. One of the aforementioned artists who will remain anonymous spoke of Jerry Lee in less than flattering terms. After working on the tour with the Killer, he discovered that Jerry Lee is "A real rouser." He reported also that one night in Sydney, Jerry Lee had propped his shoes up on an antique coffee table in the hotel lobby. When the manager kindly asked Jerry Lee to remove his feet from the table, he just looked up and didn't move one inch away from the prized table. Also, early in the morning, pants, shirts and even shoes would be left outside their doors for the cleaning lady to pick up and Jerry Lee among some of the others would steal and hide them away.

When I attended a private bash at Jerry Lee's Hotel Muehlebach Suite in downtown Kansas City, his southern friends (Jerry Lee's version of the Memphis Mafia) were there in force and they inadvertently found out that I had made a tape of his Gold Buffet concert appearance in North Kansas City. Jerry Lee's lieutenant's forced me into a bedroom and told me that Jerry Lee did not want me to walk out with that tape. They pressured me into selling them the tape for five dollars. I assured them that I knew it was illegal to tape a concert but I was only going to play it for personal use only but my pleas found only deaf ears. "You caught Jerry cussin' on tape and he doesn't want his image tarnished," said one close associate who made me play part of the tape back for him.

Throughout the years, Jerry Lee Lewis has had many problems. A major worry for him occurred in 1959-'60, when his version of "Old Black Joe" was released on Sun. Jerry Lee was banned once again from the airwaves, especially in the South, because of the racial overtones that the record supposedly contains. (The first time that Jerry Lee was banned from radio airplay was due to the 1958 marriage to his third cousin, Myra Gail Brown that raised the ire and eyebrows of the British and American public at the time. As a result of Jerry's wedding vows, a one-hundred thousand dollar tour of Europe was cancelled and his records were blackballed from the states as a result of marrying such a young woman.)

In 1961, Jerry Lee Lewis made one of the finest recordings of his entire career with the Ray Charles composition of "What'd I Say." The flip side, "Cold, Cold Heart" even made Hank Williams, Junior a fan of Jerry Lee. He told Jerry Lee in Memphis back in the sixties that his daddy, Hank Senior, would have been proud of Jerry Lee's updated version. "Cold, Cold Heart" featured Jerry Lee's crisp and clear vocal dynamics with a piano solo full of sugar coated staccato trills that was brisk and lively and was never short from brilliant.

During a 1964 tour of Great Britain where every venue Jerry Lee played at was a sell-out, the Killer admitted that he was "The Fifth Beatle" and realized that they had blown a hole through the musical lid. The British newspapers at the time reported that Jerry Lee was drawing even bigger crowds than the Beatles!

But, two years later, in an interview with a British fan in England, Jerry Lee candidly admitted that he had disdain for the British Beat groups such as the Beatles and the Rolling Stones—"You mean (do I like) the group's and things? Naw, I don't like them. If you put them (Stones, Beatles, etc.) all on one stage (together) at the same time, they'd all sound the same." Jerry Lee also felt at the time that the Beat scene of the mid-sixties would be a lot more interesting if there was variety offered — "If you get a variety of entertainers over here, it would be better — ."

The Killer (as he calls other people and also has used "Tiger" in name-calling his fans, associates, etc.) has been known to pull off some real boners with his band while performing. While playing at the Gold Buffet in Kansas City in September, 1982, Jerry Lee was starting a song he hadn't played in a long while, "She Still Comes Around (To Love What's Left Of Me)." After starting the song out in the key of E instead of the intended key of G, Jerry quickly cupped his right hand on his face and laughed at his right hand man, guitarist-fiddler, Kenny Lovelace and jokingly exclaimed in his ear, "I started that song in the Key of H—my hemorroid key."

Possibly the most notorious incident in the Killer's wild lifestyle is that infamous fateful day when he arrived in front of the Graceland mansion in his limousine with a loaded revolver under his console. It was reported that Jerry Lee surprised the guard at the front gate by demanding to see Elvis. According to Kenny Lovelace, Jerry Lee was innocently caught by the Graceland security guard and the police—"Elvis called Jerry Lee to come over. After Jerry arrived at the gate, he told the guard to notify Elvis that he had arrived. Jerry had the gun legally in his car and that was all there was to it. What initially happened was that there was a mixup. Jerry had his car radio turned up so loud that he didn't notice what was happening around him when the guard had called the police and they surrounded his car."

Jerry Lee's headaches have followed and plagued him into the 1980's. He was accused (but later acquitted) of killing two of his last three wives and the IRS has issued a lien against Jerry Lee's property in Nesbitt, Mississippi. Also, he had a perforated ulcer problem while on tour in Ireland in the spring of 1985. Miraculously, he is a survivor like a cat with nine lives.

His problems continued to mount on July 13, 1985. While the Band Aid Concert for Africa was taking place on two continents, Jerry Lee Lewis in contrast was making an appearance at the Ozark Inn at Excelsor Springs, Missouri, that very same day. However, he was an hour-and-a-half late for performing as a result of Clay County assistant prosecutor James H. Thompson Junior's acting as a bill collector, confiscated thirteen hundred dollars from Jerry Lee. Jerry Lee supposedly owed fifty-one thousand dollars to a Charles Cowan for concerts the Killer contracted to make in Kansas but didn't show up for in 1980. Kerrie, Jerry Lee's current wife, claimed that security was lax when Thompson and his assistant used illegal rough-house tactics in frisking money off of Jerry Lee. They unbelievably attacked this timeless rock legend by unethically trying to pull jewelry from his fingers and wrists. Coincidentally, while the rock charity concerts in London and Philadelphia were garnering money for the starving children of the world, the authorities in this small modest midwestern town were busy snatching money as well as jewelry away from the personal body of Jerry Lee Lewis which only left him with six-hundred and fifty dollars in his pocket only for the IRS to grab onto later.

In spite of bad publicity, ex-wives, the IRS, health problems and lawsuits chasing him, Jerry Lee Lewis still amazingly rocks on.

Joey Dee's "Peppermint Twist" in 1961 made him a national institution that year. His group, the Starlighters, were appearing with him at Forty-fifth Street in New York where the elite of high society and many movie and recording stars came to be seen by newsmen and columnists alike. This was the era of the Twist dance and Chubby Checker was its King while Joey Dee was the Prince of a movement that is in large part responsible for separating couples from such contact dancing as the Jitterbug.

Because of his popularity at the Peppermint Lounge, Joey wound up in two movies, "Hey Let's Twist," and "Two Tickets To Paris."

After several more chart successes, such as "Shout," "Roly Poly" and "Mash Potatoes (Part one and two)," and a highly sellable live album appropriately called "Live at the Peppermint Lounge." (Whereby the aforementioned songs can be heard), Joey Dee came up with solo effort minus the Starlighters in the teen ballad that asks the big question, "What Kind Of Love Is This."

In 1963, Joey Dee and the Starlighters toured parts of Europe and Scandinavia where he helped introduce the Twist to new audiences overseas. It was during that tour of Sweden that the Beatles opened the concert shows for Joey Dee and the Starlighters.

Because of all the rigors of the road, Joey Dee's first marriage ended in divorce. His second marriage has had more longevity since he has included his wife and daughter in his group.

Joey's first record, "The Rain" for Little Records occurred long before he recorded "The Peppermint Twist." "I know of only one person that has it," he once said.

Explaining the early demise of his career in 1964, Joey bluntly admits that "The British Invasion of 1964 is what hurt us American artists but it didn't last very long."

Joey Dee's musical influences in his earlier life happen to be many of the singers that came out of Harlem and the rest of New York (his home town) during the fifties. "I always followed the black artists like Willie Winfield and the Harptones than any other type of music," claims Joey.

Joey Dee's biggest regret is that he didn't cut a song that Henry Glover, president of Joey's past label, Roulette, brought to him to record. "I was in Miami and I heard this song and thought it wouldn't do anything. The song was "Crimson and Clover" and it of course later became a monster hit for Tommy James and the Shondells."

Joey Dee and his musical family still perform in and around the New York City area on rock revival shows and club dates.

There were many other artists and groups that jumped on the bandwagon due to the early sixties Twist craze. Hank Ballard who originally wrote and recorded "The Twist" was praised by Dick Clark on American Bandstand as the true originator of the popular dance style and Ballard got to lip sync his record on the dance program. Louis Prima and the Las Vegas swinging aggregation of Sam Butera and the Witnesses cut an album that couples could Twist to, while his wife and partner, Keely Smith also recorded an album of Twist songs. Ray Charles also had a Twist album and even the Beatles and the Isley Brothers cut one of the biggest Twist tunes of all time in "Twist and Shout," which was written by the latter-mentioned group in the early sixties.

After the Twist, there were other dances galore that came about in part from the many dance forms being previewed and performed on American Bandstand. Some of these dances included the Monkey, the Watusi, the Frug, the Madison, the Continental, the Dog, the Funky Chicken, the Frog, the Bird, and many more.

Johnny Cash started out as a teen idol before actually becoming a country and western star. His hits for Sun Records actually fared better than most of the label's other artists. Johnny's smash recordings were a long impressive list that were popularized between 1957-60 in "I Walk the Line," "I Guess Things Happen That Way," "Next In Line," "Ballad of a Teenage Queen," and "Fulsom Prison Blues."

It was an ironic coincidence, that this singer who sang white American Folk ballads in a hillbilly manner for the rednecks and the blue collar working class would be a marked man for marrying a woman of a Spanish decent, Vivian, who was unjustly accused of being a publicity seeking negro woman. The Ku Klux Klan was convinced that Vivian, Johnny's first wife was actually a black woman or a mixed breed outcast. Johnny and his wife unfortunately went through numerous death threats and malicious obscene phone calls. Finally, all this trouble subsided when Johnny publicly stated more than once that Vivian was indeed an Hispanic. The FBI (Federal Bureau of Investigation) was ultimately called in to investigate the Klan's illegal and unjust harassment of the young couple.

Johnny Cash, along with Warren Smith and Carl Perkins, toured the Midwest in 1962. Johnny's own headlining set was a versatile act that also included a wild imitation of his buddy and former Sun labelmate, Elvis Presley.

Johnny made a comeback on the charts in 1985 by recording in the studio with his pals—Willie Nelson, Waylon Jennings and Kris Kristofferson. However, Johnny will be most remembered for his biggest sellers of all time in "I Walk the Line," "Fulsom Prison Blues," "Sunday Morning Coming Down," and his Grammy-winning 1969 novelty classic, "A Boy Named Sue."

In the late sixties, Carl Perkins was wallowing in the gutter. Finally, after many years of boozing and doping were taking their toll, Carl disgustedly threw his whiskey bottle into the ocean and decided to clean up his act. There was a reason to feel better about himself because "Country Boy's Dream" on Dollie was a hit for Carl in March, 1967. The record reached the top twenty country lists and helped boost his drawing power as a performer.

Carl also worked through the years with his friend and former Sun stablemate, Johnny Cash for many years and even was Johnny's lead picker for a while.

In 1968, Carl was thinking about venturing out more on his own again. He was willing to book the Rocktones (my own group) as his road band.

Carl holds the honor of being the only white artist that had his original compositions recorded by both Elvis ("Blue Suede Shoes") and the Beatles ("Matchbox Blues," "Everybody's Trying to be My Baby," and "Honey Don't") who recorded Carl's songs for their "Beatle's 65" album on the Capitol label. "The Beatles have helped me a lot," said Carl in 1968. "I made over five thousand dollars (initially) in royalties from (The Beatles) recording my songs. I am deeply flattered that they did them.

"The Beatles held a surprise party for me in this big mansion in London—they held it in my honor. The guard at the door didn't recognize me and turned me away, but Ringo came to my rescue. They all sat in a circle around me and gave (me) a guitar and had me play my songs," Carl said gleefully.

In February, 1971, Carl Perkins made an historic appearance with his old friend, Bill Haley at a Rock Revival (Volume Five) concert promoted by Richard Nader at Madison Square Garden in New York City.

Carl also cut a scorching promotional LP, "Live at the Lone Star Cafe (New York City)" that found him returning home to his original rockabilly roots and early Sun recordings by performing "Matchbox Blues," "Honey Don't" and his original classic, "Blue Suede Shoes."

Carl recently has been touring the states and Europe with his two sons in his band and also endorses Apollo Hair Systems in televised advertisements.

Carl briefly appeared in the new 1985 "Blue Suede Shoes" video that celebrates the fiftieth birthday of the late Elvis Presley.

Carl has also done some acting and was last seen falling out of a building with David Bowie in a scene from a new Bowie dramalogue.

By 1962, southern rockabilly warbler Wanda Jackson was the foxiest sex kitten in rock and roll.

Since 1957, Wanda was billed as "The Singing Doll." Her first thrust of popularity came by appearing regularly on Red Foley's country music program, "Ozark Jubilee" which originated from Springfield, Missouri. On the strength of her very first hit recording, "You Can't Have My Love" for Decca Records, Wanda made many personal appearance tours that included the 1958 Auto Show which previewed the top new models for that particular year. Wanda was in good company as she co-starred with Louis Armstrong, the Royal Teens ("Short Shorts" fame), the Crew Cuts, Roger Williams, and Margaret Whiting.

This dark-haired leggy voluptuous beauty from Oklahoma City, Wanda became also known as the "Queen of the Female Rockers" by 1962. Wanda had signed a recording pact with Capitol Records by 1960 and her legendary rocker, "Let's Have A Party" climbed the charts and it turned out to be her finest waxing ever. On the strength of her hit, Capitol also issued an album by Wanda appropriately titled, "There's a Party Going On," and "Rockin With Wanda," which are both worth over eighty dollars a piece on the record collector's market.

Although "Let's Have A Party" was thought by many listeners to be the voice of Brenda Lee, it was Wanda's raspy growls on the waxing that enhanced her stardom at the time.

The "Party" single and album gained Wanda numerous personal appearance tours around the country in 1962 with her band, the Party-Timers. Her appearance at Genova's Chesnut Inn in Kansas City during that year kept the KC hot spot packed night after night. Dressed in her sensuous bright red-frilled lace dress, Wanda was all woman, brighter than life itself churning her own hits as well as those by Elvis ("Jailhouse Rock"), George Jones ("White Lightning"), and Ray Charles ("Sticks and Stones").

Wanda's apparent disdain for Jerry Lee Lewis was never any more obvious that wintery evening at Genova's when she announced that "Whole Lotta Shakin' Goin' On," the song was introduced just before tearing into the number, was actually a Little Richard song (Richard had a cover on "Shakin" too but the Commodores and Jerry Lee were the first to record and popularize it). Wanda simply refused to recognize the fact that "Whole Lotta Shakin' Goin' On" was Jerry Lee's all-time biggest seller.

Ms. Jackson's Party-Timer drummer seemed as if he was blind (he could have been) as he was wearing dark sunglasses and a mod suit behind his Ludwig drum set while playing the skins with his new felt-tipped drumsticks without missing a single beat. The other three members of the Party-Timers never miscued on her playlist of songs that also included "Cool Love" and "In The Middle Of A Heartache." The lead guitarist's sharpened shrill licks kept the audience spellbound and they kept clapping for more.

During the last set, Wanda announced that Capitol had released a new LP, "Two Sides of Wanda" and she proceeded to romp through some of her own favorite selections from the album including "Long Tall Sally."

During the late fifties and early sixties, Wanda Jackson was known to live in the rock and roll fast lane by dating some of rock's better known luminaries including Rick Nelson and Elvis Presley. Consequently, rock's early sixties sex siren gained some notoriety from many of her fiery relationships.

Wanda has the distinction to be the very first rockabilly female artist to have a longer term contract with one of the top Las Vegas niteries. In 1960, the sparkling beauty was signed to a two-week engagement at the

Golden Nugget. Because of her exciting energetic performances and the ovations she received, Wanda netted a long term contract with the Las Vegas hot spot that extended through 1961. Bill Greene of the Nugget at the time stated that "Wanda's brilliant presentation with her vibrant and projecting personality and the top quality unit, the Party-Timers, that she carries with her, will mark this as one of the best shows we have ever presented to the public at the Golden Nugget. We term Wanda and her Party-Timers as a smashing success here in Las Vegas."

In the 1970's, Wanda's scorching rockabilly rhythms were replaced with gospel selections on the Word label. Wanda burned her so-called sinful past by leaving it all behind her and renewed her faith in God and was born-again. She now looks worn around the edges from her rigorous years of traveling on the road but Wanda hasn't lost her luster for life. She's like a diamond in the rough—still shining as radiantly as ever before.

JIM HALSEY   WANDA JACKSON   Capitol

The parallel career-wise between Elvis Presley and Conway Twitty are many fold. Both of them first cut their initial demo's for Sam Phillips of Sun Records in Memphis during the mid-fifties. Their music hinges in the similar direction both of them took in the golden era of rock and roll as Conway's first released Mercury sides were "Shake It Up," "Maybe Baby," "I Need Your Lovin' " and "Double Talk Baby" were highly infectious rhythm sides that were stewed up for the label in 1957-58. These rockabilly-rocker cuts were similar to the very first records that Elvis recorded for Sun. Conway turned to pop ballads in "It's Only Make Believe," "Lonely Blue Boy," "I'll Try," and "The Story of My Love" in 1958-59, while Elvis also cut ballads like "It's Now Or Never" in 1960. They both were also consummate entertainers who went to great lengths in putting on a grade "A" show on stage. Elvis and Conway would shake it all over and their vocal technique was close to each other's mode of presentation with that distinctive deep guttural growl that became a trademark for them. Other comparisons include their movie roles as actors and their love for country music as well as crossover selections they recorded and made hits out of for each of the respective labels that these two southern born and bred artists were affiliated with.

When Conway Twitty eventually met Elvis in his Royal Suite at the M-G-M International Hotel in Las Vegas during the early seventies, he was flabbergasted by El's warm reception and hospitality. As Conway first entered through the doorway and came within the King's view, Elvis slowly got up from his chair and methodically walked toward Conway with his right arm and hand extended for a handshake while singing "People see us everywhere—," the opening strains for Twitty's number one 1958 offering, "It's Only Make Believe," which reportedly a Presley favorite.

Conway Twitty could rock with the best of them in 1959. He was a bundle of human dynamite on stage while pounding through his MGM rockers like "Hey Little Lucy," "Mona Lisa," and his remake of the Irish folk tune, "Danny Boy." His talent was never more recognizable than all of the Saturday night hop appearances he would make on a semi-regularly basis at the Frog Hop in Saint Joseph, Missouri. Conway, along with his drummer, Jack Nance and bass player, Joe Lewis would rock the large ballroom that would be continually filled to near capacity to see Conway and his group, the Lonely Blue Boys, in action.

Conway was an excellent guitar player in his own right which is something that has never hardly been mentioned before. He would play a candy apple red Gretsch guitar and sting his notes with very high energy zest and pinpoint accuracy.

There was a small incident that happened to me while watching Conway and his group perform in Saint Joseph at the Frog Hop one night in 1960. His other lead player was right in the middle of a lead break when he looked right at me and for some unknown reason gave me the finger. I overlooked the rude jest on his part and remained a fan of Conway's for over twenty-six years now.

In 1962, Conway and his band were playing a teen dance at the Armory in Atchison, Kansas, when he announced to me that he was retiring from rock and going into country music. His face lit up like a christmas tree as he exuberantly was thrilled at the prospect of the move into country. "I am tired of rock and roll and want to go into country music now," he exclaimed. "I love Hank Williams as he is my favorite and enjoy doing his songs like "Jambalya." The future for me is definately in the country and western field. I am signing up with Decca Records to sing country."

As a genuine white rocker, Conway had his biggest succession of hits for one year in 1960. He also turned to singing ballads that year more than any other time in his past with "Lonely Blue Boy," "What Am I Living For," "Is a Bluebird Blue?" and "What a Dream." Conway's big charted rocker in 1960 was his cover of the Jerry Lee Lewis hit, "Whole Lotta Shakin' Going On," which he arranged in a different way by molding the number into a slower four-four shuffle beat instead of the fast four-shuffle beat arrangement that Jerry Lee structured out for the now rock and roll standard.

Conway (whose real name is Harold Jenkins) since 1958 has had more number one hits than anybody else including the Beatles and Elvis Presley. He has achieved the unprecedented feat of having forty-six number one records to his fold as that number increases from the present into the future. The main distinction to be made is that Conway was able to pass all of the above and even Frank Sinatra also by placing most of his number one songs at the top of the selected category of the country charts.

Conway Twitty has always been a consummate business man who like Paul McCartney and Freddie Cannon was among the first in his early part of his career to invest his earnings from music in a wise and thrifty way. Conway was also the first rock artist to invest in a food line product, the Twittyburger.

Conway throughout the years have developed a solid fan club following and his various fan club chapters are among the biggest in country music fandom.

His recorded duets with popular country vocalist, Loretta Lynn, helped them both careerwise by racking up many number one hits including "After the Fire Is Gone" and "Louisiana Woman, Mississippi Man."

Little Richard Penniman admits to starting nearly everyone in the rock and roll field from 1955 on—"I'm a Quasar—a star with shouts of energy," he exclaimed. "I've been shouting for years! ! !—I started Pat Boone, James Brown, Joe Jex, Jimi Hendrix, Don Covay, Titus Turner—it was hard for people to play black original records. They had white singers cover all black records and made them popular instead of our own records—it was called Race Music at the time, but I was the first black artist to cross over."

Little Richard was uniquely talented and hit the fifties mold as a rock pioneer as much as Chuck Berry or Buddy Holly did. A former dish washer for the Grey Hound Bus Depot in his home town of Macon, Georgia, Richard quickly climbed to the top of rock's hierarchy in 1956 and became influential to all those that followed him. While touring England in 1964, Brian Epstein, the manager of the Beatles, invited the "Georgia Peach" over to meet the Mop-Top foursome of the ballroom in Liverpool—"Brian told me that they would be thrilled to meet me." Richard also exlaimed that Epstein offered him fifty percent of The Beatles take if he would just come and pose with the band—Richard turned him down. "I didn't think they was going to make it—Paul, I thought could, but not the rest of them."

One of the biggest last harrah concerts involving Little Richard occurred at New York's Madison Square Garden with Wilson Pickett, Arlene Smith and The Chartels, The Platters, The Flamingos and Chuck Jackson.

Richard sang all his hits, "Long Tall Sally," "Good Golly Miss Molly," "Lucille" and his only hit ballad, "Send Me Some Lovin."

The crowd was thrilled when Richard jumped on top of a speaker during "Rip It Up," and immediately stripped off his shirt, jewelry and threw them all out to his followers while his White Hippie drummer excitedly kept shaking his long blond locks of hair without losing a beat.

Little Richard's last movie was "Let The Good Times Roll," a film documentary dealing with Richard Nader's rock and roll revival shows. After the movie, Richard made more guest appearances on The Tonight Show and proclaimed, "Oh my soul, I'm back," he said.

But as of 1980 Little Richard, for the second time in his career, retired from rock and went into the ministry. Richard's gusty harsh vocal gospel selections are now served up for the Lord.

White soul singer, Wayne Cochran, who now sings gospel offerings, once made the following statement of Little Richard—"He comes from a generation of rockers that would go to any lengths (or extremes) to gain applause and satisfy his audiences (in performing), even if it meant walking and crashing right through into a glass door—do it! Even if it meant bleeding to death—do it!"

In the very first actual rock and roll book ever published that chronicled the early top stars in 1958, editor Vik Fredericks also included in "Who's Who in Rock and Roll," a singer by the name of Little Reboy. This Little Richard look-a-like was the spitting image of the Georgia Peach and it could easily be concluded that Reboy was none other than Little Richard himself. In the aforementioned text, Fredericks was quoted as saying the following about Little Reboy—"—Dynamic delivery—this super-charged cat rolls with the cool sensation."

In the last thirty years, there have been many imitators of Little Richard including Detroit rocker, Bob Seger and rhythm and blues turned country stylist, "Big" Al Downing.

Throughout the history of rock and roll, there is only one artist who can be called Little Richard and this wild screamer turned gospel singer-preacher has to be considered the top bronze rocker of all time.

Tommy Sands who was once married to Nancy Sinatra and had a hit for Capitol Records with "Teenage Crush" in the fifties, actually was an Elvis follower and imitator of sorts that really didn't make that much of a splash with the public as far as his longevity of hits are concerned.

Sands eventually gave up singing and headed for Hawaii. But, to prove that he still had some life in his voice, Tommy returned to a singing career and launched a musical revue for the Ramada Inn circuit in the late seventies. Tommy Sands was actually an early product of the first generation of rock and roll but surprisingly hailed the Beatles as the greatest of all time. He even went so far as to feature an entire Beatles set by staging arrangements and costumes around the "Sgt. Pepper's Lonely Hearts Club" theme. Tommy's show was complete with a chorus line of scantily-clad dancing girls that also included a flashy colorful baton twirler.

Tab Hunter and Sonny James both had a hit with the same number, "Young Love." The bulk of Hunter's recordings came in 1959 when a total of four releases were issued that year. Tab's biggest fifty-nine seller was "I'll Be With You In Apple Blossom Time."

Johnny Ferguson had two solid recording years in 1959-'60 and came up with his own swing-ballad, "Angela Jones" (MGM). After Ferguson's run on the charts, Troy Shondell helped in carrying the "Teen Idol" tradition with his 1961 smash, "This Time."

In 1959, Ray Sharpe preceded Wilbert Harrison ("Kansas City") with his own whining rock-shuffle sound with "Linda Lou" for Jamie Records.

Other solid hitmakers that kept on rocking in the late fifties through the early sixties were Lou Christie, Tom and Jerry (Simon and Garfunkel), Joe South, and gymnastic back-flipper — Curtis "Pretty Little Angel Eyes" Lee.

Rock and Roll Instrumentals were an influential style of popular music that came to form in 1959 with the Wildcats' "Gazachstahagen" on United Artists while Joey Hill and the Strangers busted out with one of the best instrumentals of all time with "Rockin' Rebel." Frank Virtue and his group, the Virtues, appeared on American Bandstand in 1959 when they performed their hit, "Guitar Boogie Shuffle." The Champs of "Tequila" fame toured the states in fifty-nine and their crazy antics that included the saxophonists jumping around and honking their horns all through the inside venues off stage and even playing while all the time following each other outside into the streets and untimately back in and finally on stage once again.

Link Wray's Cadence recording of "Rumble" was followed by a revolutionary original sizzler in the pre-psychedelic guitar rocker in "Raw Hide." The aforementioned number was released on Epic Records and was followed by an instrumental that had distortion sounding effects in "Comanche." Link wiggled and shook while appearing on American Bandstand which was likened to the style of Elvis Presley in performing his new Swan disc, "Jack the Ripper" in 1963. Link's guitar techniques were very much an influence on a young Pete Townshend back in the late fifties.

The Big Beats were another great tour band that recorded "Clark's Expedition" for Columbia Records in 1959. This instrumental unit also backed up several artists at record hops in 1959 with Sonny James, Tony Bellus, and Paul Peek. Their other discs such as "The Big Beat," "Rush Me," and "Sentimental Journey" failed to generate any interest solely because the Big Beats were stale in comparison to other recordings being released at the time. On the other hand, the band's live sessions made the Big Beats a completely different sounding aggregation than they were on vinyl. The group would play the popular songs of the day and turn them into their own vehicle. The Big Beats at record hops would break into hits like Fabian's "Tiger" and "Harlem Nocturne" by the Viscounts. The saxophonist of the combo wailed and cut loose on some soul-stirring riffs that would sting a bee on "Honky Tonk" and "Crossfire."

As the Philadelphia artists like Fabian and Frankie Avalon got more stronger in popularity, and the Twist became the teen dance rage, the Big Beat's public appearance schedules dwindled down and eventually they all got out of the ever-changing music business by the skin of their teeth and ultimately landed themselves some secure paying day jobs instead of night gigs.

Duane Eddy was the man with the twangy guitar that out-polled Frank Sinatra, Elvis Presley and virtually everybody else as the top artist in England during 1959-'60.

Originally from Corning, New York, Duane and his family moved to Phoenix while he was still in his pre-teens.

Duane's first recording was on the Phoenix-based Ford label with "Movin' 'N' Groovin' " which was sent to Harry Pinfer, the president of Jamie Records in Philadelphia. Duane was signed to an exclusive contract with Jamie and Lester Sill and Lee Hazelwood continued to write and produce Duane's subsequent hit recordings in "Rebel Rouser," "Cannonball," "Ring Of Fire," among others Duane's deep-seeding lead work on his Gretsch (later Guild) guitar was uniquely identifiable in that he played the lead string parts on the top bass strings. Duane's guitar fury was unleased with the rambunctious "Ramrod."

Throughout his career, Duane Eddy's quiet unassumed shy personality was evident in his concerts around the states as he projects a faint smile. But his natural good looks made him a perennial winner with his audience.

"The Lonely One" by Duane was a landmark recording with its medium-slow chalypso instrumental style complete with bongos as percussion. The song was debuted on Dick Clark's shows. "Yep" was Duane's next hit and the number was named after Gary Cooper's famous three letter movie drawl.

While my family and myself were on a rough and rocky forty mile unpaved stretch of road on the Colorado-Utah border at Dinosaur National Monument, we were probably the only tourists actually experiencing Duane's titled description of this instrumental that was being previewed on Denver's KIMN at the time in 1959 called "Forty Miles Of Bad Road." His next hit in October, 1959, was the shortest hit instrumental ever on record in "Some Kind-A Earthquake" which lasted barely over one minute in length.

Duane Eddy got into the movies by 1960 in Dick Clark's film, "Because They're Young" and later acted in yet another flick which was a western about Calverymen in "A Thunder Of Drums."

Duane's last hit occurred in 1963 when he cut "Dance To The Guitar Man" for RCA. The song also included an all-girl chorus that backed him in the studio for reasons of commercial appeal in order to help the record sell.

Duane Eddy has remained in the studio as a track artist for other singers including Jackie DeShannon ("Put A Little Love In Your Heart") and B. J. Thomas ("Rock and Roll Lullaby").

Next to Duane Eddy and the Rebels, Johnny and the Hurricanes were the most popular of all the rocking instrumental bands. This group from Toledo, Ohio featured the honking tenor sax wails of Johnny Paris, while close buddy, Dave Yorko punched out the hard-driving guitar riffs and got support with the intense organ rhythms of Paul Tesluk. Their solid fast tempo instrumental jumpers made the group rock and roll headliners in 1959. Johnny and the Hurricanes' biggest hits were "Crossfire," "Red River Rock," "Reveille Rock," "Beatnik Fly," "Down Yonder," "Sand Storm," and "Rockin' Goose."

Johnny Paris tried to contact Richard Nader, who promoted Rock and Roll Revival live concerts in and around the New York City area in order to be rediscovered and booked by Nader. Unfortunately, like Mark Dinning earlier, Nader didn't respond to any of his phone calls.

Johnny and the Hurricanes actually first became headliners when they toured the record hop circuit in the Midwest during October, 1959 with Skip and Flip, Roscoe and His Green Men, Freddie Cannon and Sandy Nelson.

One of their tour stops was the Frog Hop Ballroom in Saint Joseph, Missouri where Johnny and the Hurricanes played their top instrumental favorites and also helped back Freddie ("Boom Boom") Cannon.

Freddie Cannon (whose real name is Anthony Picariello) likes for his audiences to work along with him and that unforgettable night in Saint Joseph was no exception. He belted out his hits, "Talahassie Lassie," and "Way Down Yonder In New Orleans" on stage while clapping to the beat with both hands and arms elevated high over his head. (Freddie still performs today and he likes Huey Lewis and the News (he helped inspire them) and credits Chuck Berry as the true King of Rock and Roll.)

Skip (Clyde Patton) and Flip (Gary Paxton) sang their two hit songs at the Frog Hop in "It Was I" and the most popular Doo-Wopp bar song of all time— "Cherry Pie." Drummer, Sandy Nelson backed Skip and Flip during their particular set.

Roscoe and his Green Men actually were the forerunners of Kiss, Alice Cooper and Ozzy with their bizarre hair styles that were dyed green. The Green Men set the Frog Hop Ballroom on fire with their crazy antics by throwing their guitars around and playing rock and roll instrumentals including Roscoe's original offering in "Wild" that was recorded for Twentieth Century Fox.

(Epilogue — 1963)

In November, 1963, I had an appointment with a black jazz-rhythm and blues saxophonist for my first lesson on this instrument with him in Saint Joseph.

It was a pretty overcast day as I drove down a side street near the city's river front. It was in the early afternoon when I arrived at his front door step. When the door opened, Lenny and his wife Zelda were in tears—"President Kennedy was shot and I can't go on with your lesson," he sadly exclaimed. "All the hopes of my people are now erased. We're still chained by slavery. He was going to save us and now there is no hope—no hope at all." As I departed from the tenament, Walter Cronkie sadly verified the shooting and informed the American people that the worst had happened—"The president is dead." This is the way that pre-Beatle 1963 ended.

It was the calm before the storm (President Kennedy's assassination and the British-Beatles invasion of January, 1964) throughout much of 1963 when music was still music and like ice cream, there were many varieties of flavors to choose from—Jazz, Ballads, Latin-Rock (e.g.—the Bossa Nova), Limbo Rock, Pop, Country, Hillbilly, Blues, Rhythm and Blues, Hootenanny, and the newest fad that came out that year was the swirling sounds of Gospel Pop music.

The biggest Gospel Pop hits in 1963 were "The Love Of My Man" by Theola Kilgoro, "Pushover" by Etta James and Dinah Washington's "Soulsville." Gospel Pop mixed the slick polished vocals and music variations to that of a bluesy black man's raw and gutsy preaching utterances that he or she feels in a song.

Pop Gospel or Gospel Pop can also be described as another key element in rhythm and blues recordings. This music trend was being heard by over-flowing patrons at New York's Sweet Chariot. This Manhattan venue used to rock with tambourines and call and response shouts of encouragement by the audience. Celebrities used to assemble there and pack the place including Paul Anka, Dina Merrill, Brenda Lee, and Richard Chamberlain. Columbia Records magnate, Dave Kapralik was quoted as saying that "Pop Gospel is the hottest new sound and will be on the charts before the end of the year (1963)."

Unfortunately, it was the British Invasion that cancelled out that prediction. America might have won the Revolutionary War but it lost in the battle for mega bucks and chart popularity that changed the course of popular music forever. American artists like Mark Dinning whose teen ballad, "Teen Angel" later became the anthem song for Sha Na Na and others said it better than anyone — "The Beatles wiped us out."

The year 1963 was the peak popularity of Beach music and Surf-Rock instrumentals. Frankie Avalon and busty Annette Funicello were seen on screen making out on the beach while James Darren was chasing Gidget.

Because of the popularity of sun and surf on the teenagers of America, water sports were in vogue that year when rock and roll instrumentals such as Surf-Rock became a hot sound like the likes of such southern California bands as the Routers, the Surfaris, the Chantays, the Challengers, Dick Dale and the Deltones, and of course, the Ventures with their own version of the Surfari's original hit, "Wipe Out" which has become the most recreated suft instrumental of all time. The Beach Boys and Jan and Dean continued with their very own brand of surf-styled hits while on dry land in Missouri, the Rocktones had local surf instrumental rockers on the Kansas City-based Damon label in "Hightime," "The Rocktones Twist" and "Rumblin'." These Surf-Rock sounds included a swooping fast picking guitar riff attacks with a high treble and vibrato bottoms.

Dick Dale was the "King Of The Surf Guitar." His album, "Surfer's Choice," set the standards for other rock guitarists. Dick Dale also has the honor and distinction of being the only rock star to have appeared in a major film with the late legendary sex goddess Marilyn Monroe in "Let's Make Love."

Dick has always been an avid surfer and was picked along with his group, the Deltones, to co-star with Frankie Avalon and Annette Funicello in "Beach Party."

Dick's interest and love for animals and his affinity for them stimulated a desire to create a zoo-like house filled with an ocelot, a cheetah, a baby ape, a Great Dane, parrots, a boa constrictor and dozens of other pet pets.

In a 1981 interview, Dick Dale explained how animals and the California Surf have a distinct relationship with his own guitar stylings: "I have handled and trained a five hundred pound Bengal Tiger." Although he has been mauled and mangled, Dick maintains a firm attitude that animals are more trustworthy with their own feelings and more honest with another animal or mammal than humans are: "I trust animals over people. They don't bullshit you—they either like you or hate you—there is no in-between. As opposed to humans, you know where you stand with animals. Animals are more honest. My style of playing comes from man and beast coming together in the surf. I visualize the beast such as the Bengal Tiger and the mountainous waves of the surf crashing together with such an intensity that it all overpowers you." Dale further emphasized that this is the way his sweeping guitar riffs are imaginatively created for all of his past, present, and future Surf-Rock recordings.

In the late seventies, a New Wave journal featured Dick Dale in an article that had him quoted as saying the following about New Wave and Punk Rock music — "They got to put them all in a cage and gas them." After the article was subsequently published, Dale paradoxically became a hero to the Punk-New Wave movement. "After I said that, they thought that was "Cool" and praised me as actually one of their own. They have called me the "Granddaddy of Punk," he jokingly exclaimed. "The B-52's have patterned after me," he quipped.

Dick Dale not only was a musician's musician, but he was a teacher. He taught the late legendary rock guitarist, Jimi Hendrix how to play many of his glistening riffs. Dick plays the guitar left-handed without reversing the strings and Hendrix picked up this technique and utilized it himself. Dick Dale relates that "Hendrix used to stand in front of me and watch me play for hours."

Dick in the 1980's has now gone into semi-retirement from performing. He is involved full time in his own business interests in southern California including two night spots known as Rendezvous One and the Rendezvous Two.

Water sports were synonymous with Surf music such as Body Surfing and Water Walking.

Water Walking back in the summer of 1963 was done with water shoes along with a good sense of balance. The shoes were made of a resilient plastic compound coated with fiberglass mat and resin. Foot wells in the middle of the shoes lowered the participant's center of gravity to give any water walker a better balance. Rubber thongs, similar to those utilized on water skis, held he or she's feet into place, but was released quickly if anyone happened to capsize. Everyone simply slipped their feet into the shoes and started walking.

Besides surfing and its musical heroes, 1963 was also a year for some unforgettable memories in the annals of popular music. Trini Lopez was predicted to be "The Spanish Elvis" while televisions two most famous doctor's, Vince Edwards and Richard Chamberlain caused their fans to run to their real physicians for hearing and indigestion problems due to the short-lived recordings that both of them made which included syrupy off-key ballads.

If that wasn't enough to give anyone an Excedrin headache, Doris Day's son, Terry Melchior, Columbia's rock and roll producer in '63, supervised the session of his mom's recording, "Let The Little Girl Limbo"— "Uugh!" Doris Day's recording was an obvious spin-off (or rip-off) to Billy Bland's "Let The Little Girl Dance."

Dion DiMucci was the biggest male singer of 1963. He also became a producer for the very first time that year when he produced "Feeling No Pain" by the Del Satins. The Del Satins took over where the Belmonts left off as Dion's back-up group on all of his post Dion and the Belmonts material.

On January 12, 1963, country music songwriter-vocalist, Willie Nelson married Shirlie Collie from Chillicothe, Missouri. His wedding which took place in Las Vegas, occurred at the time that Willie was appearing at the Golden Nugget with his wife-to-be. The wedding party was a bit unusual. Willie's steel guitarist, Jimmy Day, was best man; Paul Buskirk, beard and all, was "matron of honor," and a third member of Willie's unit, Johnny Bush, was "flower girl."

When Willie married Ms. Collie, he was cutting records for Liberty. He was tagged with the title "Mr. Progress" for his ability to write progressive but very understandable country songs. His earlier self-penned tunes included "I Fall To Pieces," "Crazy," "Hello Walls," and one of the most recorded of all the Willie Nelson songs in "Funny, How Time Slips Away." The latter song has been recorded by nearly everyone and his brother. Willie once explained the reason for the number's timeless popularity: "It is basically a simple song," admits Willie. "I think it's simplicity helped in its longevity."

Before the Beatle's Capitol disc, "I Want To Hold Your Hand" took over Bobby Vinton's "Blue Velvet" as the number one song on the Billboard charts, there were actually even earlier signals that the British invaders were coming. The first publication in the states that mentioned the Beatle's surging popularity was the November, 1963 issue of Teen Scene magazine. It was also announced by a foreign correspondent that Jerry Lee Lewis, Roy Orbison, Duane Eddy, Connie Francis, Bob Luman, and Brenda Lee were slaying their fans at Beat shows all over Great Britain in the fall of '63. It was also officially reported from a survey taken by Teen Scene prior to September of that year that the three most popular teen idols of the day were Cary Grant, President John F. Kennedy and astronaut, Gordon L. Cooper. "Isn't that a surprise?" remarked an editor of the teen publication who disclosed the findings of that poll.

From the 1963 gossip mills, Tuesday Weld reportedly gave up her beatnick look and started dressing "properly" again. Natalie Wood was dating Warren Beatty and it was quickly publicized that Frank Sinatra wears toupees in his movies. Fans of Elvis Presley was surprised to learn that their hero's latest films were financial failures and that is why Ann-Margaret was originally signed as his leading lady in El's planned movie, "Viva Las Vegas." "Sexy Annie's supposed to fire things up," commented a columnist who wrote for a teen gossip magazine. The biggest financial disaster of 1963 was from the silver screen as "Cleopatra" became a red-inked forty million dollar failure.

Actually, without knowing it, Dick Clark's autobiography summed up 1963 in the book's title — "To Goof or Not to Goof."

PROFILE OF AN UNKNOWN GREAT ROCKER

Little Richard — goin' wild, Madison Square Garden, New York City, N.Y. 1973

Various pictures of Jerry Lee Lewis through the years 1959-'76

Wildest action shot of Jerry Lee Lewis ever taken—Grandview, Mo. 1965

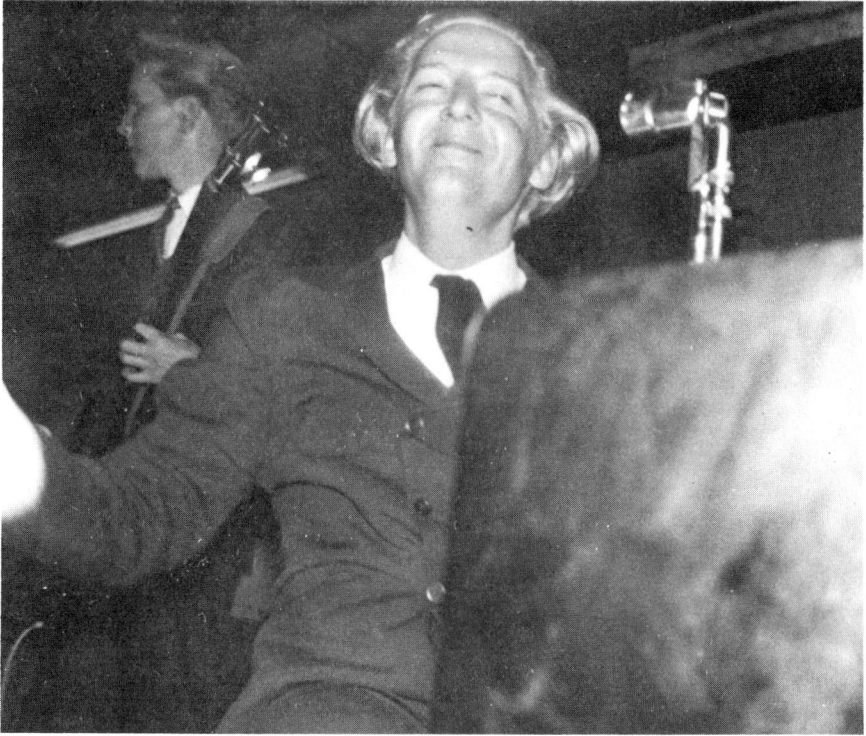

The Killer in rare form — Grandview, Mo. 1965

CHUCK BERRY

CHESS ™

Above – Chuck Berry in action (Kansas City, 1973). **Below** – Chess promo picture of Chuck

Rare picture of Screamin' Jay Hawkins in concert — England
in the mid-sixties

Top—the late great Patsy Cline. Bottom left to right—Rockabilly star from Virginia—Randall Hall, Dottie West, Carl Smith, Claude Grey, and Memphis Rockabilly—the late Lloyd Arnold

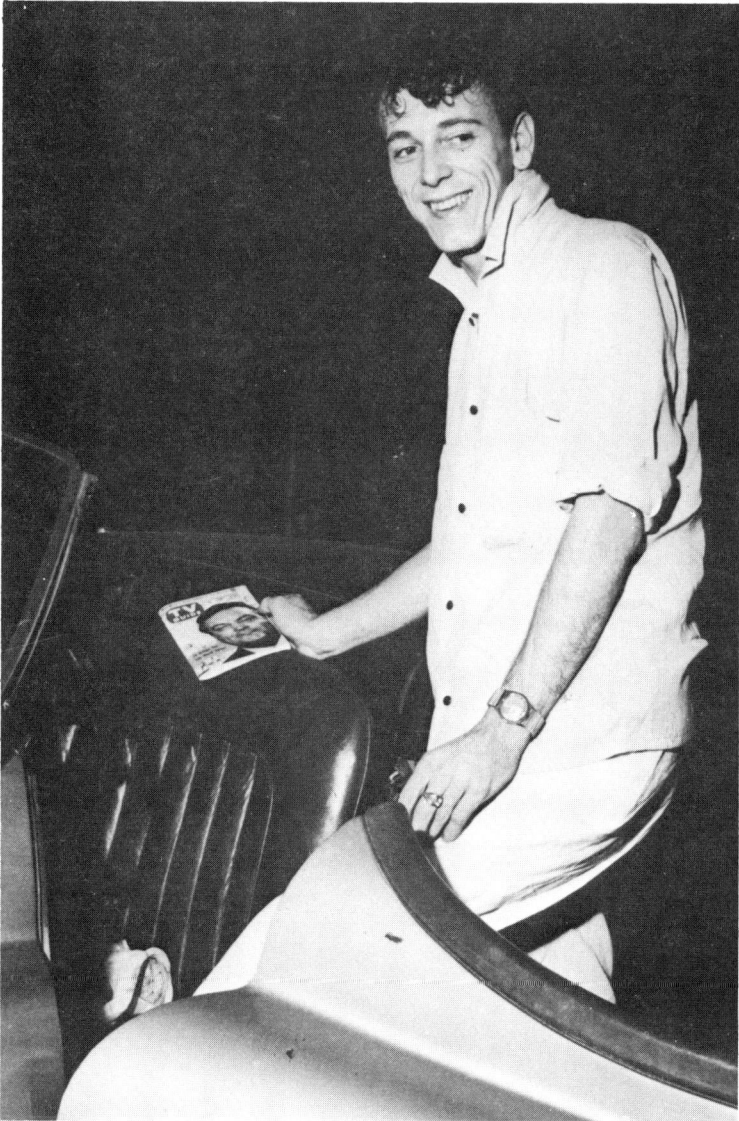

Rare picture of Gene Vincent holding a copy of TV Guide (Jackie
Gleason on cover)

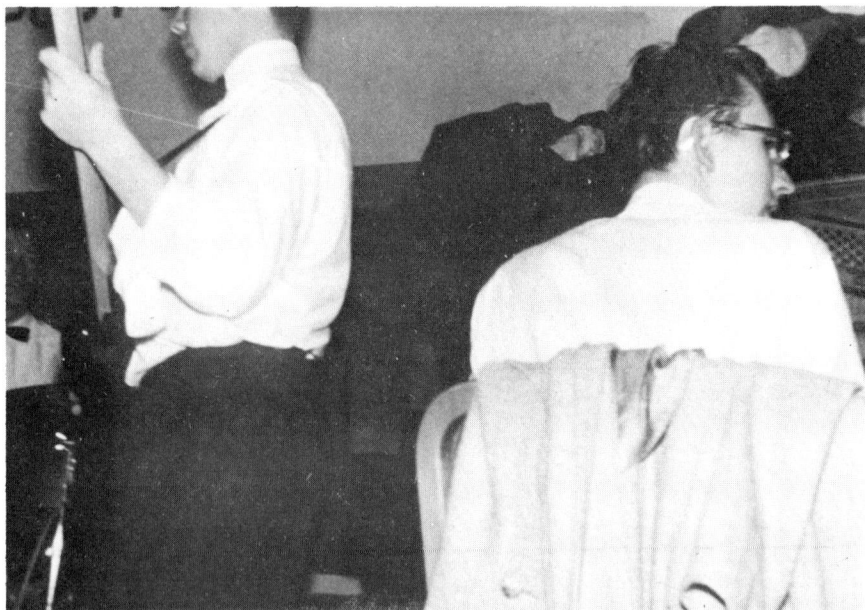

Gallapin' Cliff Gallop and his revamped Blue Caps Band (1960) note pianist Buddy Holly look-a-like

Johnny Cash imitating fellow Sun stablemate, Elvis Presley, Kansas City (1962)

Rare rebel pose of Elvis taken by himself in a photo booth just before he
started his fabulous career with Sun and later RCA Records. More pictures
of Elvis in concert in next pages

Conway Twitty in action—Frog Hop Ballroom (1959) with his group, the Lonely Blue Boys. Drummer Jack Nance, co-author of "It's Only Make Believe"

Conway Twitty in action (1959)

Wayne Cockran in Action — 1973 (note hair of C.C. Rider saxist in action standing up on end)

Lloyd Arnold and his idol — "the Possum" — George
Jones. Below — Johnny Cash and the Tenn. Two

1950's Rockabilly-Rocker, Pat Kelly (rare fifties promo picture shown here)

The Big Beats in Action – St. Joseph Mo. Crystal
Ballroom circa 1959 rockin' up the house

Above—clockwise Roscoe and his Green Men, Skip and Flip, drummer Sandy Nelson and Johnny and his Hurricanes

Above—Freddie "Boom Boom" Cannon—St. Joseph, Mo. (1962). Below—Rod
Bernard and Bobby Vee

The Champs show poster above (note Glen Campbell in picture) below — with Seals and Crofts (1959)

Clockwise from top—Bellnotes ("I've Had It" fame) backing the Dupress—Electric Theatre, St. Joseph, Mo. (1959), "Teen Angel" Mark Dinning, various souvenir early 60's r'n'r show pictures

The Twistin' Parkettes (above). Singer Dee Dee Kinnebrow of the Crystals (below)

THE PLATTERS

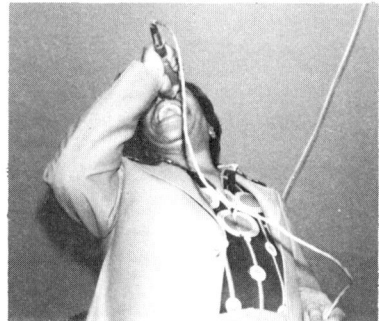

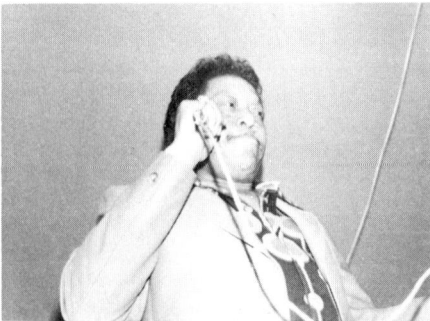

Above Bunker Hill (The R & B Man). Below B. B. King and Bobby "Blue" Bland

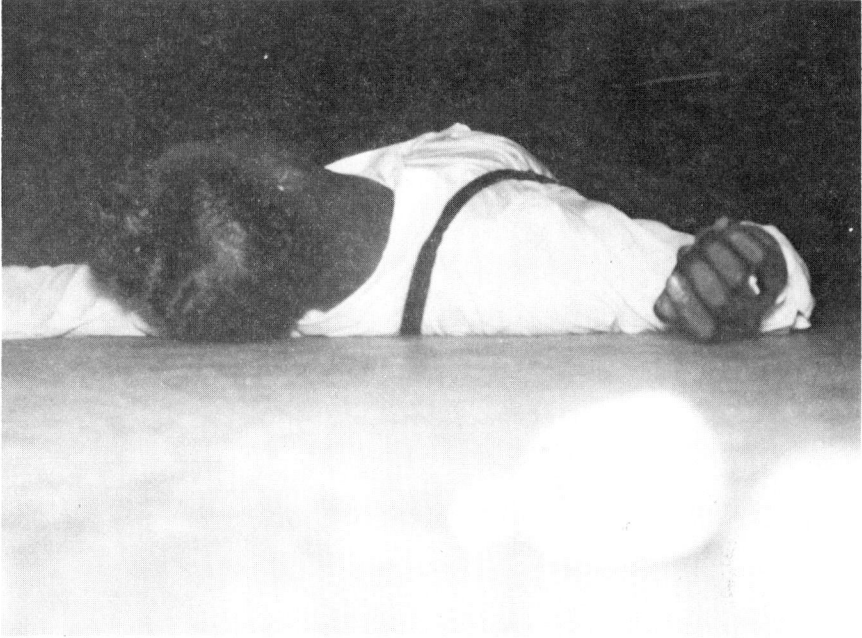

"The Jackie Wilson Show" (1962) Kansas City, Missouri Auditorium an unforgettable experience

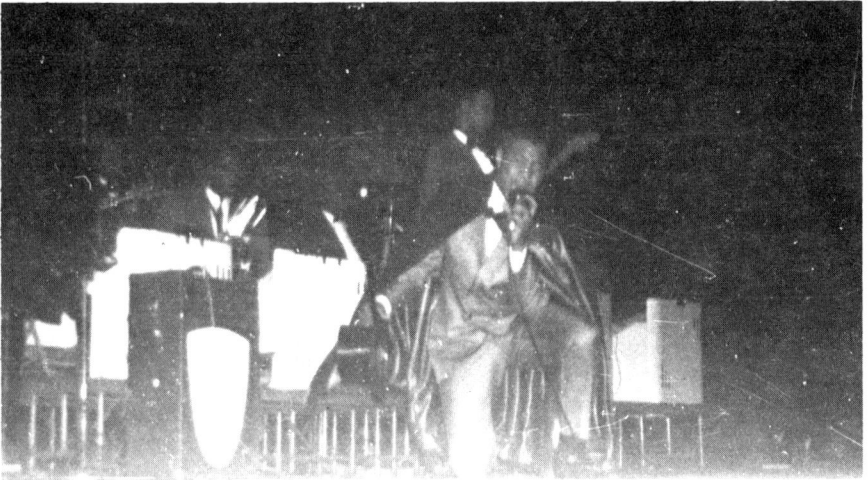

The Spinners (above) and Gene Chandler as "The Duke of Earl (1962). Below — Elvin Bishop goofin' around with female admirer Tanya Tucker after car accident

Arlene Smith of the Chantels — backstage at New York's Madison Square Garden (1973)

Saucy picture of Tina Turner (right) on the Sonny and Cher Show singing with a sexy Cher

The fabulous Diana Ross performing at Kemper Arena, Kansas City, Mo. (1978)

THE DRIFTERS

MERL LINDSAY
and
his
OZARK JUBILEE BAND

Compliments of
Frank Lowe GE 2-8717
Frank Lowe CE 9-9600
Chester Amos WI 3-3646

TALENT AGENCIES
311 S. KLEIN ST.
OKLA. CITY, OKLA.

The Teenkings

Managed by
ROBERT AYERS ORCHESTRAS

SHAKIN' STEVENS

Epic

Gorgeous George in action. He almost lost his pants and has to hold them up in leap (lower picture)

BUDDY HOLLY & THE CRICKETS   BH2L · © BHMS 1976

These two Buddy Holly pictures are used by permission and courtesy of Buddy Holly Memorial Society through Bill Gripps — Thanks Bill!

RICK NELSON
And The Stone Canyon Band

Eddie Cochran (1938-1960) — A Legendary Rocker

PROFILE OF AN UNKNOWN GREAT ROCKER

Charlie Heinz was a white boy who tried to sing in a soulful black manner in the late fifties. Charlie sang at local rock shows in the midwest during 1960 with Gene Vincent's ex-guitarist, Gallopin' Cliff Gallop (prior to playing with Heinz, Cliff had just finished his last tour with Vincent just before "Mr. Be Bop A Lula's" departure to England).

Although he didn't have any hits, Heinz always brought the house down with his wild stage shows that resembled a cross between Gene Vincent, Gorgeous George and Jerry Lee Lewis. He would start a song like "Be Bop A Lula" with a Gene Vincent growl and then purposely fall down and furiously squirm all over the cold hard floor like a mad man unleashed from a straight jacket. In person, Heinz sang Elvis and Jerry Lee Lewis-styled rockers. But on vinyl, the opposite was true as Charlie's label, Satellite was trying to mold him into a balladeer. Charlie, along with the Anita Kerr Singers, cut the calypso-ballad, "Destiny" in 1959. The song was very close in resembling Paul Anka's "Diana."

Heinz peddled his records himself at all his record hop appearances.

After being complimented for his showmanship at a record hop sponsored by local station KUSN in St. Joseph, Missouri during 1960, Heinz simply admitted to his watchful admirers that his frenzied stage routines should be considered taboo and off limits for anyone to try. "I wouldn't recommend what I do to anyone," he honestly stated.

Touted as the next Gene Vincent, Heinz didn't really survive the music scene after 1960.

JERRY LEE LEWIS
AND HIS BAND

Jan. 21 & 22   9701 S. 71 Hiway

— CLUB 95 —

Adm. $2.00   Friday Night Only

FEB   65

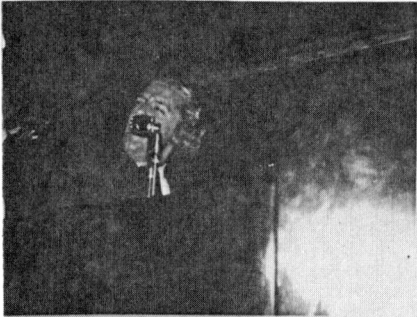

FEB   65

GENOVA'S CHESTNUT INN

2800 E. 12th   Kansas City, Mo.   BE. 1-9696

Dancing Every Night to the Music of
JACK HENSLEY and the REBELS

The "Big" Names Only in the Country and Western Music
Field Come in Person to Chestnut Inn Every Week.

Schedule of Coming Attractions!

Dec. 19 thru 22—JERRY LEE LEWIS
One of the most fabulous entertainers of the past
decade. Doing those Big Numbers that only Mr. Lewis
can do, "Whole Lot of Shaking Going On" and "Great
Balls of Fire." For a jumping good show, this is the
one. Plus a very fine Jumping Band.

Jan. 2 thru 5—HANK THOMPSON
America's No. 1 Western Swing Band. Hank Thompson and the Brazos Valley Boys will once again help
us celebrate our anniversary. This is the 29th year
of continuous operation of Genova's Chestnut Inn,
under the same ownership and in the same location.
For this reason we wanted the best to help us celebrate and the Best Band in the Land is Hank Thompson and the Brazos Valley Boys under the fine leader-
ship of Billy Gray. FREE RECORDS will be given
away on Wed., Jan. 2, and Thurs., Jan. 3.

FOOD SPECALS

Your choice—lb. steaks - Sirloin - T's	$2.90
Your choice—½ lb. Steaks - Sirloin - T's - Fillet	1.50
½ Fried Chicken	1.25
Spaghetti and Meat Balls	1.00
Bar-B-Q Ribs—Long Ends....$1.50 Short Ends....	1.75
Italian Steak Sandwich	.65
Ham or Beef Sandwiches	.50
Hamburgers ....40 De Luxe	.50
Cheeseburgers ....45 De Luxe	.55
French Fried Shrimp or Oysters	1.25

The JERRY LEE LEWIS
International Fan Club

CORDIALLY WELCOMES

Bob Kinder

AS A MEMBER

Kay Martin

KAY MARTIN, PRESIDENT S   REPRESENTATIVE

GENOVA'S CHESTNUT INN

2800 E. 12th   Kansas City, Mo.   BE. 1-9696

Schedule of Coming Attractions!

Nov. 14 thru 17—GEORGE JONES
Now Geo. Jones with his own band. Doing all his All Time Hits, "White Lightning," "Window Up Above," "Why! Baby Why," "Aching, Breaking Heart," and his newest, "She Thinks I Still Care." Voted the Number One Country Singer by Cash Box for 1962. We love Geo. in Kansas City. This is our boy and he's home, so don't you dare miss this.

Nov. 23 and 24—FARON YOUNG
C & W Music's finest voice doing his all time big hit, "HELLO WALLS." Faron and his band, "The Country Deputies," are the greatest entertainment unit out of Nashville for many years. Some recent good releases have been "Backtrack" and "Congratulations" and "Love Has Finally Come My Way."
Friday and Saturday Nights Only.
Be sure and make reservations.

Nov. 28 thru Dec. 1—DARREL McCALL
This fine young Grand Ole Opry star has the number three song on the C & W Charts today, "Dear One."

Dec. 5 thru 8—CONWAY TWITTY
This Fabulous Rock and Roll and Country Music Combination Man is one in a million. Doing his great hits, "It's Only Make Believe" and "Comfy and Cozy." Conway is a country boy at heart and wishes to do half of his show in country music style.

Dec. 14 and 15—ERNEST TUBBS
The "King of Country Music" will be here with his very fine band, The Texas Troubadours. Ernest Tubbs has so many hit records that we can't begin to list them here. If you like country music then this is the Top Show you will see and hear this year. Friday and Saturday nights only. Make reservations.

OCT • 61

"SOUND TRACK FIVE"
THE
VETERANS ADMINISTRATION
MONO CUT
Time 4:30
33⅓ RPM
Program No. 555 The Beatles
Program No. 556 The Don Ellis Show
Program No. 557 The Jud Strunk Show
This recording is the property of the Veterans Administration and cannot be broadcast under commercial sponsorship
APPROVED BY AFM
72200—1
ATLANTIC RECORDING STUDIOS
11 WEST 60TH STREET, N.Y.
THE BOBBY DARIN
THE LADY CAME FROM BALTIMORE
BMI
45 RPM
ATLANTIC
PAIN
NEAL FORD AND THE FANATICS
Produced by: Jones Productions
CLIFF SHEPHERD
KEEP IT A SECRET
CHOIC
502
R-207
NOT FOR SALE
Knox Music Inc., BMI
Time: 2:48
PROMOTION COPY
FOOT RACE
(Frank Frazier)
FRANK (SHAKE APLENTY) FRAZIER
OUR RECORD LABEL KANSAS CITY MISSOURI
Special
BEARCAT BLUES
SE JACKSON
Time: 2:43
U-250
Since his sensational rise to fame with I LOVE YOU YES I DO, Moose Jackson has been touring the country with his own unit, "The Buffalo Bearcats," playing the country's finest theaters, ballrooms, and clubs.
Instrumental
4551
(K8181)

BRIEF SUMMARY

The dangerous practice of "hazing" in American schools, frequently headlined in newspaper stories, is given a dramatic expose in Metro-Goldwyn-Mayer's "Platinum High School," starring Mickey Rooney, Terry Moore and Dan Duryea, and introducing popular singer Conway Twitty in a straight dramatic role. Co-starred are Warren Berlinger, Yvette Mimieux and Jimmy Boyd.

The new picture is permeated with both suspense and fast action in its story of a father (Mickey Rooney) who investigates the mysterious death of his son at an exclusive military academy for wealthy delinquents, situated on a remote island.

Highlight scenes include a three-against-one fight with rifles (one of the most savage and realistic ever depicted on the screen) and the story's climax in which a speedboat attempts to run down the occupants of a small outboard motorboat in shark-infested waters.

An Albert Zugsmith Production for MGM, produced by Red Doff and directed by Charles Haas, "Platinum High School" was filmed largely on location at Catalina Island.

CAST

Steven Conway	Mickey Rooney
Jennifer Evans	Terry Moore
Major Redfern Kelly	Dan Duryea
Billy Jack Barnes	Conway Twitty
Crip Hastings	Warren Berlinger
Lorinda Nibley	Yvette Mimieux
Bud Starkweather	Jimmy Boyd
Hack Marlow	Richard Jaeckel
Joe Nibley	Jack Carr
Charley Boy Cable	Harold Lloyd, Jr.
Vince Perley	Christopher Dark
Harry Nesbit	Elisha Cook, Jr.

An Albert Zugsmith Production. Produced by Red Doff. Directed by Charles Haas. Screen Play by Robert Smith. Based on a story by Howard Breslin. Released by Metro-Goldwyn-Mayer.

YVETTE MIMIEUX WINS AWARDS HANDS-DOWN!

Yvette Mimieux, Metro-Goldwyn-Mayer's fast-rising starlet, currently appearing with Mickey Rooney and Terry Moore in "Platinum High School," is rapidly becoming Hollywood's "Award Queen."

In 1957, the blonde actress was named "Miss Harbor Day." 1958 brought her the title of "Los Angeles Art Directors' Queen." During the same year, she became "Los Angeles Boat Show Queen." In 1959, she was named "National Electric Week Queen" and Yvette's most recent title is "Hollywood Deb of the Year."

CATALINA ISLAND ONE OF THE STARS OF MGM'S "PLATINUM HIGH SCHOOL"

One of the most versatile performers in Hollywood history is Catalina Island.

Cast in many roles over several decades of filming, Catalina, off the California coast, has "played" the part of Pago-Pago, Barbados, the coast of Spain, even New England's Cape Cod. The island has such a variety of scenery that it assumed each locale with complete conviction. And just to prove how attractive it is without "make-up" and in its own right, on at least two occasions, Catalina has appeared as Catalina Island on the screen.

Currently it is seen as the dour and menacing Sabre Island in Metro-Goldwyn-Mayer's "Platinum High School," starring Mickey Rooney, Terry Moore and Dan Duryea. Rooney goes to the island as a young father investigating the hazing murder of his son at a school for wealthy delinquents. The last time he made a film at Catalina was in 1953. The island played itself and Rooney appeared as a rollicking, carefree bachelor sailor. Tempus fugit.

One of the pioneering movie location jaunts to Catalina Island was made in 1923, when Director Maurice Tourneur took silent picture stars Anna Q. Nilssen and Milton Sills there for scenes in "The Isle of Lost Ships," with Catalina impersonating the eerie shores of the Saragossa Sea. The following year, Catalina played itself under the direction of Cecil B. DeMille in "Feet of Clay," with Rod La Rocque and Vera Reynolds.

Director James Cruze needed pickup shots for the buffalo stampede in "The Covered Wagon" in 1923. Instead of treking back to the Southwest, he shipped J. Warren Kerrigan, Lois Wilson and a herd of buffalo to Catalina for a sequence. Cruze and the actors left when the scene was completed, but the animals remained and their offspring still roam the island.

The craggy coastline of the island impersonated Cape Cod in 1924 in "Women Who Give," starring Frank Keenan and Barbara Bedford. The same year, Catalina substituted for Barbados in the West Indies for "Captain Blood" which brought J. Warren Kerrigan back to the island, this time with Jean Paige.

Maurice Tourneur took Anita Stewart and Bert Lytell to Tahiti for "Never the Twain Shall Meet." But after the company's return to Hollywood, it was decided additional sequences were needed and Catalina graciously became the village of Papeete.

The island's coastline posed as the shore of Tripoli for "Old Ironsides," with Charles Farrell and Esther Ralston. It became Pago-Pago for Gloria Swanson's production of "Sadie Thompson."

THE ADDITIONAL SCENE AND PLAYER MATS, SHOWN IN THE COMPLETE CAMPAIGN MAT ON ANOTHER PAGE, MAY BE ORDERED SINGLY.

One of the early "talkies" to be filmed at Catalina was "The Narrow Corner," starring Douglas Fairbanks, Jr. and Patricia Ellis, with a South Seas atoll locale. It became an island in the Dutch East Indies for "Typhoon" (Dorothy Lamour and Robert Preston); a French penal colony for "Condemned" (Ronald Colman and Ann Harding); the coastline of the Bay of Monaco for "My Past" (Bebe Daniels and Ben Lyon); Singapore for "Scarlet Seas" (Richard Barthelmess and Betty Compson).

Called upon to appear as the coast off Spain, Catalina obliged in "Blockade," starring Henry Fonda and Madeleine Carroll. It played the title role in "Treasure Island," with Wallace Beery and Jackie Cooper, then switched to the role of Tahiti in "Mutiny on the Bounty," which starred Clark Gable, Charles Laughton and Franchot Tone.

Catalina Island has had as notable a film career as any glamour star. And it's been a longer career than most other "actors" can boast.

$500,000 Shark Accident Insurance Policy!

Because of shark casualties off Pacific beaches, Producer Albert Zugsmith took out a $500,000 accident insurance policy on Mickey Rooney and Terry Moore during filming of Metro-Goldwyn-Mayer's "Platinum High School." The stars spent a week on scenes which had them swimming in deep waters off the California coast after a speedboat chase ends in disaster.

Statistics disclose that the temperature of the Pacific Ocean off California has risen ten degrees in recent years, with the result that man-eating sharks have been attracted to waters where they never before have appeared.

Tough Role For a Girl Who Doesn't Even Smoke

Terry Moore claims she most difficult acting assignment career in Metro - Goldwyn - Mayer's "Platinum High School," in which she stars with Mickey Rooney and Dan Duryea.

Terry, a member of the Mormon Church, who neither smokes nor drinks, portrays a chain-smoking, vodka swigging girl in the new film.

"Producer Albert Zugsmith co-operated with me in respect to having my cigarettes for the film denicotinized," Terry explained, "and, of course, the vodka actually was water. As a consequence, when the cameras turned, I had to rely on sheer imagination!"

The ALL NEW—

KUSN
TOP 50

WEEK OF _____ April 3, 1961

DRINK Coca-Cola

1270 kc

THE OFFICIAL RECORD OF ST. JOSEPH BASED ON RECORD SALES, JUKE BOX PLAYS · · · AND · · ·

YOUR REQUESTS TO

KUSN's
Big
3
DJs

L & M

JIM MEEKER

RICK MORGAN

#	Title	Artist	Label
1.	On the Rebound	Floyd Kraemer	RCA
2.	Surrender	Elvis Presley	RCA
3.	Don't Worry	Marty Robbins	Col.
4.	Apache	Jorgen Ingmann	Atco
5.	Wheels	Billy Vaughn	Dot
6.	Gee Whiz	Carla Thomas	Atl.
7.	Call Me Anytime/All of Everything	Frankie Avalon	Chan.
8.	Ebony Eyes/Walk Right Back	Everlys	W-B
9.	Lazy River	Bobby Darin	Atco
10.	Blue Moon	Marcels	Colpix
11.	Stayin' In	Bobby Vee	Lib.
12.	Where the Boys Are/No One	Connie Francis	MGM
13.	You Can Have Her	Roy Hamilton	Epic
14.	Find Another Girl	Jerry Butler	V-J
15.	One Mint Julep	Ray Charles	Imp.
16.	Your One and Only Love	Jackie Wilson	Bruns.
17.	Pony Time	Chubby Checker	Park
18.	Asia Minor	Kokomo	Fels
19.	Runaway	Del Shannon	B-T
20.	For My Baby/Think Twice	Brook Benton	Merc.
21.	Hearts of Stone	Bill Black	Hi
22.	Baby Sittin' Boogie	Buzz Clifford	Col.
23.	Second Time Around	Frank Sinatra	Reprise
24.	Ja-Da	Hurricanes	B-T
25.	Portrait of My Love	Steve Lawrence	UA
26.	Aint That Just Like a Woman	Fats Domino	Imp.
27.	A Hundred Pounds of Clay	Gene McDaniels	B-T
28.	Model Girl	Johnny Mastro	Coed
29.	Tunes of Glory	Cambridge Strings	London
30.	Ram-bunk-shush	Ventures	Dolt.
31.	Little Boy Sad	Johnny Burnette	Lib.
32.	Just for Old Times Sake	McGuires	Coral
33.	Take Good Care of Her	Adam Wade	Coed
34.	Dixie	Duane Eddy	Jamie
35.	Good Time Baby	Bobby Rydell	Cameo
36.	Big Mr. C	Link Eddy	Rep.
37.	Tonight My Love Tonight	Paul Anka	ABC
38.	Pony Express	Juniors	Swan
39.	Tenderly	Bert Kaempfert	Decca
40.	Trust in Me	Etta James	Argo
41.	Ling Ting Tong	Buddy Knox	Lib.
42.	Fell in Love on Monday	Fats Domino	Imp.
43.	Happy Birthday Blues	Kathy Young	Indigo
44.	Dedicated to the One I Love	Shirelles	Scep.
45.	One Eyed Jacks	Ferrante & Teicher	UA
46.	Theme from My Three Sons	Lawrence Welk	Dot
47.	You Can Depend on Me	Brenda Lee	Decca
48.	Some Kind of Wonderful	Drifters	At.
49.	Sweet Cathy	Ray Peterson	Dunes
50.	Puh I Do	Clarence Henry	Argo

Coke makes your party sparkle

DRINK Coca-Cola

HOWDY COUSIN! DON'T MISS JOHNNY AND THE HURRICANES--THE NATION'S
#1 ROCK & ROLL ATTRACTION --AT THE EAGLES BALLROOM THIS FRIDAY
NITE. So fellas, you TICKETS AT DOOR ONLY. ADMISSION JUST $1.25.

THE BIG REC—Hi-Fi CLUB
Brought to You by KUSN and COCA-COLA every Week

PHOTOS FROM WANDA'S SCRAPBOOK

WANDA and close friend, Hank Thompson.

WANDA's manager, Jim Halsey, sits behind WANDA and her father, Major Tom Jackson.

This picture of WANDA and Rickey Nelson was taken when they appeared together for a big show in Dallas, Texas.

picture was taken of WANDA at one of recording sessions at the Capitol Studios in ywood, California.

Another shot of WANDA in action at the Capitol Studios.

Because of her extended tours WANDA spends many hours on the telephone when she is home catching up on news of friends and relatives.

A likes to spend her time learning new licks guitar.

WANDA JACKSON!

WANDA has appeared on many tours with Elvis Presley. This informal shot was taken on one of them.

SUPERSONIC ATTRACTIONS
presents

THE JACKIE WILSON SHOW

PROGRAM

JACKIE WILSON

JERRY BUTLER

CHUCK JACKSON

GARNET MIMS
& THE ENCHANTERS

DIONNE WARWICK

THE IMPRESSIONS

MITTY COLLIER

GORGEOUS GEORGE

THE UPSETTERS ORCHESTRA

For further information or assistance on the MGM-Bantam tie-up contact:

J. J. Shapiro
Bantam Books, Inc.
25 West 45th St., New York 36, N. Y.

'PLATINUM HIGH SCHOOL' MUSIC PROMOTIONS

Conway Twitty   Jimmy Boyd

STILL NO. 762X20   STILL NO. 1762X17

For a non-musical picture, PLATINUM HIGH SCHOOL offers some of the strongest music promotion opportunities in years.

MGM Records' star Conway Twitty, with three million-seller records already to his credit, makes his motion picture debut in the film. Jimmy Boyd, another featured player in PLATINUM HIGH SCHOOL, has been a recording sensation ever since his record of "I Saw Mommy Kissing Santa Claus" was released.

Utilize the stills here illustrated of Conway Twitty and Jimmy Boyd for window displays in your local music and record stores. Tie-in with your local music stores for window displays of Conway Twitty's latest album, "Lonely Blue Boy," (illustrated at right) the title song of which has already sold more than a million copies as a single. Be certain that your local playdate copy, along with the announcement that Twitty can be seen for the first time on film in PLATINUM HIGH SCHOOL, receives prominent credit in any tie-ups.

Contact your local disc jockey and have him devote an entire show or a portion of it to favorite Conway Twitty songs and/or to Jimmy Boyd, with credit to their appearances in PLATINUM HIGH SCHOOL and to your playdate copy.

Tie-in with the TV station in your town on their teen-age dance party and have them devote a program to Conway Twitty records (a favorite of teen agers), with credit to PLATINUM HIGH SCHOOL and your playdate.

Order stills by number from National Screen.

PAT KELLY

On August 15, 1939, a son was born to Beatrice and John Kelly of Tulsa, Oklahoma. They named their new son Bobby Pat Kelly.

Pat became interested in music when he was quite young. However, it wasn't until he was thirteen that he got his first big break. It was in Glasgow, Montana, that Pat first met the public, and to his delight was accepted with open arms. Ray Price was playing a show there along with Lonzo and Oscar, Justin Tubb, and Goldie Hill. Pat went backstage during the show, and asked Ray's manager if he would let him sing a song or two on the show, and after he had auditioned, he was given the chance he had been waiting for. Pat was accepted with such a cheer, that he was asked to go on with the show for the rest of the tour. He put three Grand Ole Opry tours to his credit that summer.

Pat is now twenty years old and has moved to Nashville, Tennessee, where he is booked and managed exclusively by his father, John Kelly. Pat has appeared with all the big named Grand Ole Opry stars, and is indeed on his way to a bright new future.

Early in 1957 Pat signed a contract with the Jubilee Recording Company in New York. His first record for Jubilee was called "HEY, DOLL BABY" b/w "CLOUD 13". Then in June of '58 Pat's second recording was released. It was called "PATSY" b/w "THAT IS WHERE MY MONEY GOES". Pat's third recording will be released <u>very soon</u>, so do watch for it.

On the personal side of things Pat stands six feet tall, weighs 160 lbs., and has wavy dark brown hair, and the brightest blue eyes you've ever seen.

To sum up this brief story, it's only fair to say something about Pat's personality. It's the opinion of all his fans and many talent promoters, that he is one of the friendliest and most well mannered entertainers they have ever met. Watch for Pat and see him if you have a chance!!!

THE NATIONAL PAT KELLY FAN CLUB
MISS NANCY BRYANT-PRESIDENT
ROUTE TWO
WARSAW, INDIANA

RECORD COMPANY
PRESENTS
THE NEW SOUND

THINKING ABOUT
THE GOOD TIMES

JIMMY CHURCH
101

BLUES FOR
THE BROTHERS

JOHNNY JONES
102

THE SHOCKER

PEG LEG MOFFETT
103

SOLDIER'S
PRAYER

EDDIE BILLUPS
104

GET UP OFF IT

GORGEOUS GEORGE
105

SINCERELY

EMORY &
THE DYNAMICS
106

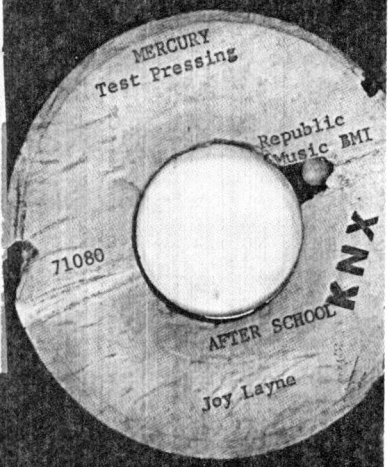

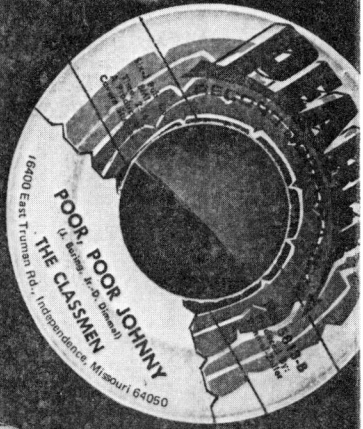

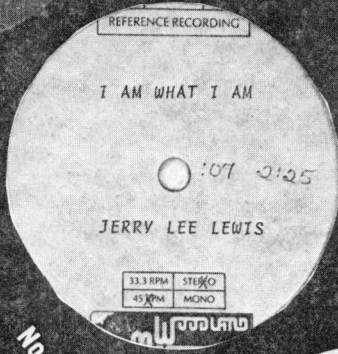

GLOBE THEATRE
Savannah, Missouri

Shows Start Monday and Friday, 7:30 P.M.; Saturday Nite, 7:00 P.M.;
Sunday Matinee, 2:00 P.M.; Sunday Nite, 7:30 P.M.

25c   FEBRUARY, 1959   50c

Sun-Mon Feb. 1-2

7th Voyage of Sinbad

The picture you have all been
waiting to see in glorious color
with Katy Grant (Mrs. Bing
Crosby)

Sun-Mon Feb. 8-9

The Reluctant Deb.

Comedy in Color
John Saxton, Sandre Dee

Sun-Mon Feb. 15-16

Defiant Ones

A very good story of two
escaped convicts, one colored,
one white,
Stars Tony Curtis

Sun-Mon Feb. 22-23

Marjorie Morningstar

Drama in color
Natile Wood, Gene Kelly
Ed. Wynn

Fri-Sat. Feb. 6-7

Naked In The Sun

Bullwhip fury in color

PLUS

Dangerous Youth

Life story of Elvis Presley

Fri-Sat. Feb. 13-14

SENIOR PROM

Lets have a ball with Louis
Prima, Bob Crosby, and
Freddy Martin's Orch.

PLUS

Sweet Smell of Success

Burt Lancaster & Tony Curtis

Fri-Sat. Feb. 20-21

JINX MONEY

Huntz Hall & Bowery Boy's

PLUS

FIRE DOWN BELOW

South American story in Color
With Reta Hayworth

Fri-Sat. Feb. 27-28

TALL STRANGER

Out-door Action in Color
Joel McCrea

PLUS

TUNNEL OF LOVE

Comedy with Doris Day

Coming Soon

FROM THE EARTH TO MOON
CAT ON A HOT TIN ROOF
WIND ACROSS THE EVERGLADES
MAN OF THE WEST   LITTLEST HOBO
SNOWFIRE   TORPEDO RUN
BIG COUNTRY

SAVANNAH REPORTER PRINT

TEEN-AGE
DANCE
SATURDAY

8 p.m. to 11 p.m.

V. F. W. HALL
St. Joseph Ave., St. Joseph, Mo.

MUSIC BY
KEN BROWN AND THE Montereys
50¢ DONATION

Gary Stites in dressing room 1969 Rocker from Colorado

LITTLE RED ROOSTER
HAS WON
THE ROLLING STONES
another silver disc
CONGRATULATIONS BOYS!

At the beginning of the rock era people like Little Richard and Jerry Lee Lewis took this on-stage exhibitionism to outlandish lengths.

Little Richard would (and still does) tear off his tie and shirt, leap about and scream his head off. Between times he produced an almost unbeatable pure rock gospel sound.

Went mad

Jerry Lee Lewis stood up to play the piano and then went mad sliding up and down the keyboard seemingly playing as though he wasn't really interested in what he was doing. Casually lifting one leg onto the top of the piano as he played.

But to both these men the way they behaved on stage was strictly for the audience. It was showmanship. Off-stage Little Richard was a preacher and Jerry Lewis a quiet thoughtful man.

Today it is different. With Mick, Wayne, Ray and the others it is not just a big act.

These people bring into the spotlight a very large part of their own character.

THE BIG BOPPER

CHANTILLY LACE

CHANTILLY LACE

BIG BOPPER'S WEDDING

DECCA
F 12014

The Decca Record Company Ltd
Decca House
Albert Embankment
London S.E.1

SOUL ON ICE—BLUES ON FIRE

The blues are the roots while soul is the tree to what has to be the two prime music forms of early rock and roll. Country and western was of course a fundamental musical form that merged with the above styles into a fabrically interwoven product that has been known today as just rock.

Soul music has been a brisk lively deep sound that carries with it all it has to offer the public including belly-busting vocals, tight rhythmic horn accompaniment, along with brisk blues licks from the guitarist, and solid driving beats from the percussionists and drummers.

There have been many forms of soul and blues offerings. Lightnin' Hopkins helped popularize the country blues—down in the gut vocals with a single acoustical guitar accompaniment; urban blues; Delta blues; and even hillbilly blues. Some of the best forms of soul have come from the creative endeavers of Stan Lewis and his Paula-Ronn label, out of Shreveport, Louisiana. Many of his top "get down" blues and "deep" soul include Ted and ("Little") Johnny Taylor, George "Wild Child" Butler, Roscoe Robinson and Buster Benton. Their recordings on Ronn and Paula represent the pleading and yearning style of basic "roots" music found in the South including gospel inspired chants along with a heavy foundation of strong-stirring intense brass orchestrated backgrounds, along with soaring deep guttural vocals, combined with solid trebled guitar chops. Other quickly identifiable forms of soul include the heavily brass foundation of Memphis soul from Stax, the slicked up Motown Sound and even the Atlantic r&b soul, all of which differs from the hemogenized diluted "whitened" soul of today found in the music of Lional Richie and the Pointer Sisters.

Before Tina Turner became the "Synthesized Soul Wonder" of 1984, Annie Mae Bullock (her real name) got her professional start twenty-seven years earlier with her former husband, guitarist, Ike Turner.

Ike and Tina both worked the chitlin circuit in and around Saint Louis as they became a touring road show with their backup group, the Kings of Rhythm and the sensuous and sexy accompanying vocalists, the Ikettes.

Ike and Tina's hits since 1959 through 1971 were far and between. Their first chart-buster was "A Fool In Love" for Sue Records that featured Tina's raspy screams throughout the song. Ike and Tina over seven years later were produced by the legendary Phil Spector on their next moderate hit in "River Deep, Mountain High." Finally, Ike and Tina scored with the duo's biggest seller ever in John Fogerty's "Proud Mary" in 1971.

In 1968, the entourage played several dates in the state of Missouri. Just like other people, Ike and Tina has had their own share of problems. Professional as well as petty jealousy involving other associates plagued them both. While in Saint Joseph, Missouri at an Eagles Lodge dance, Ike and Tina could be heard arguing back and forth from the back door of the lodge. The two of them still hung in there together and provided the small throng of Saint Joseph natives with a dazzling show.

Before "Proud Mary" became a smash for them in '71, Ike and Tina were co-starring along with fellow soul artist, Wayne Cochran and the C. C. Riders in the MGM Grand Lodge at Las Vegas in 1969. Wayne Cochran, was once called the "White James Brown" but now sings gospel songs, related years later how Ike and Tina were often staring from the wings of the MGM Grand Lounge (during the time in August, 1969, Elvis Presley was headlining the MGM's main showroom) while he and his group, the C. C. Riders, were playing their fast-paced version of "Proud Mary" complete with horn arrangements and soaring guitar solos. Cochran explained almost bitterly how "They (Ike and Tina) would be watching while my band, the C. C. Riders were playing "Proud Mary" as my orchestra would be turning the audience on by jamming on their horn solos by parading off stage and entertaining the customers by sitting on the ladies laps and would keep on playing while standing on tables and chairs and we would steal the entire show with encore after encore—and believe it or not we could not sell our version of "Proud Mary" to the record companies. The record companies said it wouldn't work—shit! ! ! With sellout after sellout and people calling us back to do "Proud Mary" again and again and the record exec's telling me it won't work."

It was of course later put to test that Wayne Cochran's "Proud Mary" arrangement would work on vinyl when Ike and Tina themselves stole Cochran's version and recorded it for United Artists Records.

Since her divorce from Ike, Tina has enjoyed a renaissance as she has become the queen of New Wave Soul and several hits to boot in 1984-85.

Sam and Dave like Ike and Tina Turner are another soul rhythm and blues duo that got their start in the late fifties but whose career didn't reach its zenith until a few years later in the sixties.

They became the purveyors of soul music with the soul anthem, "Soul Man" and the gutsy rhythmic, "Hold On I'm Coming."

Since the original Sam and Dave duo didn't jell personally, Dave (Prater) is now touring the world in the mid-eighties with a new partner, Sam Daniels. His touring schedule with a brand new partner included venues in the Midwest. Acting brash and looking more annoyed to be caught around interviewers right after a gruelling Kansas City appearance, Dave Prater seemed more interested in sipping on a beer and entertaining a cigarette than he was in what he perceives as a regimen in useless idle chatter — "I talk to so many people. Once in Miami, someone was interviewing and putting out a whole load of crap and (Sam) came out laughing. Look, I'm a businessman. I do it for the money and nothing else. It is useless and no good throwing around hot towels. You gotta learn (show) business first before you ever get into it."

Dave Prater's background is pretty easily predictable considering the style of music he has been into the last thirty years. "My family was very religious. I have a strong church background in gospel. I also grew up listening to some real stuff — blues like B. B. King, Lightnin' Hopkins and Sam Cooke. Everything they ever did I listened to and it all weaves into music for I am just going by my own influence. It all depends on your taste."

Prater reinterated once more that he doesn't have any problems with the stardom that Dan Aykroyd and John Bulushi had found in copying Sam and Dave's song and dance routines a few years back in performing "Soul Man" in the movie, "The Blues Brothers." "Soul Man" was leased to another company (Atlantic Records) so I wasn't involved with it."

Sam and Dave's dynamic sixties soul compilations stereotype that turbulent decade but their early development occurred before even 1960. "Roulette was our first label. We were there five years with them." Dave quickly boasted about the distinguished stable of rhythm artists that were signed to the New York-based company in and around 1958. "Roulette cut big jazz artists like Count Basie, Duke Ellington, Sarah Vaughn, Joe Williams—we were with the right people."

Prater was quick to shrug off the suggestions that soul music has been a forgotten phenomenon only making a comeback through race music in reverse like the Blues Brothers. "Rhythm and blues hasn't gone nowhere else. I'm not going to change. I ain't into disco or rock—none of that shit. I'm from the blues. Today's artists are using the same chord changes we did on early rock and soul classics. For example, eight-bar chord changes are essentially from the same songs. It's actually the same stuff being recycled.

"As far as contemporary trends are concerned, it's another product the majority of which is made up of electronics, gadgets, synthesizers. They're all just machines—that's where it's at. It's the money knockin'." (A confidant suggested to the aging soul man that because of drum machines, the current crop of drummers have forgotten how to play with brushes which are predominately used in soft standards and jazzy swing offerings. Bob Dylan even has stood on record against what he has called "Stale" electronically incorporated instruments that are unnaturally being used today—"The human heart doesn't even beat that way," he once opined to an interviewer.)

In spite of very few hits for Dave and the newly acquired Sam, the former's DP (Dave Prater) Productions in New Jersey keeps him busy by producing, writing and directing the talents of others. "I am chairman and president of the company," says Dave confidently as he is wearing a smile of self-recognition.

Dave's future projects with Sam are helping to bring a fresh breath of air and a spark of hope in their past sagging career. "Our 'Soul Man's' on a Campbell Soup commercial," says Dave proudly. "NCR Records in Holland is issuing a single and Polygram is doing a release. Also, there is this group that wants me to send in a recipe for a celebrity cookbook from some of my songs."

Time has a bad way of eroding the commercial longevity of any recording artist but Dave Prater is philosophical about what lies ahead of him in the near future without looking back into his not to distant past. "It was only yesterday, that's all I know." Time right now is frozen into the sixties as far as Sam and Dave are concerned as this tenacious duo are into somewhat of a soul revival.

As opposed to Sam and Dave, the Spinners have been able to top the charts and survive ever changing musical trends. Next to the Jacksons, they have been the most enduring rhythm and blues group in the last seventeen years. With numerous gold and silver album and single awards to their credit, these Detroit natives which include Pervis Jackson (bass), Phillippe "Soul" Wynn (lead tenor), Bobby Smith (tenor-lead singer), and Henry Fambrough (baritone-lead singer) have been working together for over two decades of entertaining their fans with vocal dynamics combined with sparkling choreography of well rehearsed and polished dancing skills. A fifth member, Billy Henderson is the one that was originally responsible for the unit's use of tightly-knit-choreography.

Pervis Jackson reminisced on the group's beginnings: "We went to school together in the same (Detroit) neighborhood."

"Well there was a television program that used to come on in Detroit every Saturday. In addition to all of the professional talent they would show, they would have a night for amateur complete with a first prize. We noticed that regardless of who they would have on their show, a group would always win. So, we got the grand idea of rehearsing a couple of songs to go on for that prize. We used to mess around singing but it was nothing serious. But, after going on the program and winning first prize, we started rehearsing other tunes to do other shows around town—then came the after-school dances, local clubs around Detroit."

"I don't really think that we got seriously involved until about 1961, which is the year that our first record came about in "That's What Girls Are Made For." Billy Henderson, Henry Fambrough, Bobby Smith, and myself are the four that's been together since the beginning. Phil joined us in the latter part of '71—that was the year we went with Atlantic Records. He fit the group so well that I actually feel like he's been here all along."

Pervis candidly explained the reason for the Spinner's departure from Motown (their first label). "The years that we were with the Motown Recording Company, we weren't getting the kind of records we felt we should. We would always be on other people's shows and in order for us to go out and perform we had to resort to gimmicks and things like that even back then. For example, we had an act where we called ourselves the Brown Beatles. We worked two years off just that and then we put together a thing called the Motown Impressions. We did Marvelettes, Supremes, Temptations, Stevie Wonder, the Miracles, (musical material), just to name a few. It had been a thing where it sort of became a trademark with us."

Why have the Spinners survived for so long when most others fail? "A lot of people ask how do we get along. In the Spinners there are two Taurians, myself and Henry Fambrough; two Aries which are Bobby Smith and Phil Wynn and one Leo in Bill Henderson. Regardless of what our opinions are and what each of us feels about certain things, the fact is that we are able to think "Spinners" alike. As long as we are that way, we will always continue to be around."

Tragedy befell the Spinners in July, 1984, when their beloved lead vocalist, Phillippe Wynn collapsed and died on stage in California from an apparent heart attack.

The other two black groups that have maintained longevity are the Dells from Chicago and the Isley Brothers. The latter group especially have been able to survive changing trends by flowing along with any new musical developments. The Isley's first thrush of popularity was in 1959-60 with the rock classic, "Shout," which would often be the closing encore number for many of the rock and roll shows due in part to its crowd and artist chanting call and response hollers throughout the song. The Isley's stayed on top even longer with their other original classic that also became a vehicle for the early Beatles sound in "Twist and Shout."

The Isley Brothers later formed their own label, T-Neck Records and was able to achieve much sustaining power during the seventies.

Kool and the Gang from the Philadelphia area were among the most militant of all the black groups. From "Who's Going To Take the Weight?" on Delite in 1971, and their many releases, the group's popularity still seems solid. Kool and the Gang were very openly aggressive in 1972 with a rebellious anti-white attitude. For example, in Kansas City, one of the lead singers put up his fisted right hand over his head on stage and raised the middle finger and said, "This is for you, Whitey."

The black groups and duos for the most part in rock's golden days weren't as militant as Kool and the Gang and their ilk that soon followed. The Flamingos, the Moonglows, the Clovers, Maurice Williams and the Zodiacs, including those that were discussed earlier, had a mellow "Cool" attitude—not a militant one. These artists back in rock's infancy were not out to preach hatred or to divide the races or make antagonizing social protest statements. These early groups knew what the meaning of music was all about—and that was to entertain and make their listeners feel good—not to depress them with negative empty thoughts.

Diana Ross is somewhat of an enigma. After twenty-two years of hit records, her popularity has been assured and secured in spite of the fact that the majority of the female singers that started recording over twenty years ago like Brenda Lee and Lesley Gore are no longer as popular. Ms. Ross has broken attendance records in Las Vegas and has sold well over two hundred million copies—quite a statistic since her early beginnings were humble at best.

Diana was born in the Brewster housing project in Detroit and has maintained an honest profile while living in a world of slick trouble-shooters and money hungry leeches.

Ms. Ross's first name on her birth certificate was accidentally spelled "Diana," but friends and even family close to her has nick-named her "Diana" instead of her real name, "Diane," which Motown founder and president, Barry Gordy, Junior, and most of the people that personally know her still do use, but she had preferred to stay with her mistaken first name and leave "Diana" for stage and billing purposes.

Diana Ross, Florence Ballard, and Mary Wilson first worked for Barry Gordy's Motown complex as backup studio singers. When the trio approached Gordy for a small debt he owed them, the girls were sent in the studio and at that point began their string of block-busters like "Baby Love," "Where Did Our Love Go," "I Hear a Symphony," and the list goes on.

Everything was coming up roses for the group until 1968 when internal problems began to appear. Florence Ballard was beginning to tire from playing second fiddle and backup to Diana and the wear and tear from so much touring prompted her to cancel out on a Hollywood Bowl appearance. Cindy Birdsong, a former member of Patti LaBelle and the Bluebelles, filled in at the Bowl. Surprisingly, Ms. Birdsong's strong physical resemblance to Florence made the audience unaware of any substitution. Also, it was during this period of time that Mary Wilson helped keep pace with Diana's vocal ability, in case Ms. Ross ever decided to leave the Supremes.

In 1968, Jean Terrell (sister of heavyweight fighter, Ernie Terrell) was discovered by Barry Gordy. Diana felt strongly that Jean was capable of taking her place as the lead singer of the Supremes, and this was finally an opportunity to leave and gear her status as an entertainer in another direction. Diana felt that she was heading in the path of becoming a soloist that the "public was sort of pushing me in. I followed them rather than them following me."

Although her liason with Gordy and Motown ended in 1981 when she signed a multi-million dollar contract with RCA Records, Diana still never forgot her past and the original person that first put her on top. Diana showed her appreciation to Gordy by appearing on the television special Motown's Twenty-fifth Anniversary Show. During the program's finale, Diana was seen prodding Gordy from the balcony to come down on stage and sing "Someday We'll Be Together" with some of the other guest stars including Michael Jackson, Marvin Gaye, Adam Ant, and Lionel Richie.

Diana's duet album with Julio Iglesias has ignited the rumor mill that the two of them are romantically involved with each other, as their romantically provoking love pose on the cover of the twosome's LP for RCA has suggested, and thrown fuel on the fire that has ignited the scandal sheets a la the National Enquirer and the Star to write about them.

Another great female rhythm and blues artist that has always possessed the same personal magnetism and vocal prowess of Diana Ross, but who has come up short of having as many hits as her peer is Etta James.

Etta got her initial start in show business by being discovered and appearing with her mentor, Johnny Otis. The Johnny Otis Show toured extensively in the fifties and it helped give Etta a solid start in show business.

In the mid-fifties, Etta recorded for the Los Angeles-based Modern label. Her recording of "Dance With Me Henry" gave her the opportunity of playing more lucrative dates in the LA area.

Etta later cut some more hits for Chess Records out of Chicago and her 1966 recording, "Tell Mama" was another top smash for her.

Ms. Jameses creative involvement with producer Jerry Wexler of Atlantic Records afforded her with the opportunity of signing with that major company in the mid-seventies. Her subsequent album, "Deep in the Night" became a brilliant work of art as Etta masterfully mixed colorful blends of rhythm and blues to pop melodies. For example, Etta's version of the Eagle's number, "Take It to the Limit" was awesome.

Etta complemented Tim Moore's soulful composition, "The Charmer," when she sang the tune on national television of the American Songfest contest. Her treatment and arrangement of Moore's score helped win it first prize as the top song entered in the competition.

Etta James had the distinct honor of headlining a blues and jazz concert in the summer of 1981 at the Hollywood Bowl. This was a special event as the top rated female vocalists from the two aforementioned genres were featured including such renowned legends as Sarah Vaughn, Sippie Wallace and Willie Mae "Mama" Thornton.

Always a big favorite of Mick Jagger and Keith Richard, Etta toured and opened for the Rolling Stones during their 1978 stateside show dates. It has always been known in inner music circles that "nothing goes betta' than Etta."

The real fantasy of sex and dance coming together occurred in the spring of 1962 when a premier dance troupe, Lou Parks' Twisting Parkettes from New York brought many firsts in the rock and roll ballgame. It marked the first time that a professional dance team co-headlined a touring rock roadshow that was playing the major cities nationwide.

They even have the distinction to be the first organized rehearsed dance unit to win top prize at the international twist contest held at New York's plush Waldorf Astoria and to find their way into a six weeks engagement with Lloyd Price at the Apollo Theatre. While at the Apollo, the Parkettes opened and closed all the daily shows there.

The year 1962 also brought about the very first time that a featured dance was the central theme for a rock and roll show to be utilized by a dancing group of hoofers. In this case, the twist was their featured dance that the Twisting Parkettes used in their name during the last half of the Twist craze that was making heroes out of Chubby Checker, Joey Dee and Hank Ballard.

The Twisting Parkettes excelled in combining sensuality to their own hip shaking burlesque bump and grind routines as they not only twisted but also shimmied and poured sex all over their adult oriented stage act.

It was their biography in 1962 that contained an accurate description of the dancers—"The acrobatic twisting of the Twisting Parkettes is fascinating to watch. It's amazing how limber and yet how rhythmic these boys and girls are. They work as a dance group, not just individuals."

The Twisting Parkettes actually came along years before sex and dance were performed in a somewhat theatrical setting. Eight years later, sex and dance along with rock and roll were put together into two hit rock musicals in "Hair" and "Oh Calcutta."

Although they never did cut any recordings as singers, the Twisting Parkettes biggest claim to fame was in 1962 when they did their big nationwide tour by co-headlining with two musical legends in Fats Domino and Brook Benton.

The Vibrations were the best in combining the skills of gymnastics and choreographic dance steps to song lists. Their appearance on the Murray the K rock and roll shows in New York and the Supersonic Attractions "Biggest Show of Stars" tours made them popular nationwide. The Vibrations are best known for their version of "Misty" along with "Watusi" and "My Girl Sloopy."

Throughout the late fifties and early sixties, there were other groups that combined song and dance into a sensuously delightful experience. The Marathons were sensational around the Chicago and the Washington, D.C. areas while the Volumes who recorded for Chex Records found their own stronghold to be in New York, Chicago and the Midwest. The Volumes tore Kansas City up on another big rock show in 1962. Their act included splits, flashy footwork, and other sizzling acrobatics that would leave other acts limp by comparison. The Drifters with the likes of "Doc" Green were equally as sensational as they broke attendance records by being the most popularly used unit on the rock and roll circuit between 1959-64.

Jackie Wilson has been called the Michael Jackson of the late fifties and early sixties, but it can also be recognized that Michael is the Jackie Wilson of this generation — "no one will ever realize how great Jackie Wilson was," said an admirer. "You can imitate, but you can't duplicate." The late, early sixties recording star, Ral Donner related to a friend once that Jackie had stolen the show at an Alan Freed concert in New York years ago — "Brian Hyland and all of us watched from the backstage aidelines as Jackie sweating from top to bottom brought the audience to their feet." Ral Donner had confided that he had never seen such a compelling performance as the one Jackie had given that memorable night over twenty-four years ago in the Big Apple.

It is already well documented how Jackie would slay his audiences with such dynamic delivery complete with thrills and spills of well timed back-flips, jackknifes, complete splits and spellbinding footwork that his title Mr. Excitement was always well earned.

Jackie Wilson's start in show business came right after his boxing career which was for the most part, a shortlived vocation for him. His mother's demands for Jackie to quit the ring was finally met after he had already met and won a Golden Gloves welterweight at the tender age of sixteen, by claiming to be eighteen. A year later, sporting a moustache, Jackie was accepting weekend singing jobs, by telling everyone that he was twenty-one. In 1957, after a stint with Billy Ward's Dominoes, Nat Tarnopol, a Detroit music publisher, signed Jackie to a personal management contract which finally led to a contract with Brunswick Records. Barry Gordy Jr., who later founded Motown Records wrote many of Jackie's early hits for Brunswick which in turn helped Jackie's repertoire greatly. The rest as they say is history as Jackie broke attendance records in such venues as the Apollo Theatre and the Copa in New York, the Fontainbleau in Miami and the Las Vegas

Sahara. Jackie had the unique distinction of being one of the first of the "Soul" entertainers to complete a tour of the West Indies. In the early sixties, Jackie wooed audiences on the Colgate Comedy Hour and the Ed Sullivan Show where he sang his pop-opera offering of "Night."

Jackie also headlined many touring rock and roll shows throughout the entire length and breadth of the 1960's. His natural good looks and personable style always caught the ladies eyes. His popularity almost got him killed in 1961 when an avid female fan shot him. He carried this bullet in his kidney's with him to his grave when he died in 1984. Unfortunately, Jackie never did recover from his heart attack that befell him at a Dick Clark rock revival show in 1975 at the Latin Casino in Cherry Hill, New Jersey which had left him permanently comatose in a nursing home for over nine years.

Jackie Wilson's tragic death didn't get the attention and tributes that he so richly deserved. Michael Jackson however did say a special tribute speech about Jackie at the Grammy Awards in 1984. Rita Coolidge kept Jackie's memory alive when she recorded his 1967 classic, "Higher and Higher" and gave the gold record she had earned from it to Jackie. The popular group Klique has honored Jackie by popularizing two of his best kn)wn cuts in "A Woman, a Lover, a Friend" and "Doggin' Around" which have also been made into musical videos with the former theme showing young Jackie Wilson fans tracking him down at a sold out theatre with the video actually showing edited splices of actual footage of Jackie performing on television back in the early sixties.

If Jackie Wilson would have been a white man in-stead of black, there is little doubt that he would have stood taller in the rock and roll arena than say a Mick

Jagger or even a Bob Seger. The Commodores in their tribute to Jackie was so right on when they mentioned in the song's lyrics that he took us all "Higher and higher."

Gorgeous George (not to be confused with the colorful fifties wrestler of the same name) was Jackie Wilson's valet and emcee extraordinaire throughout the sixties who would have a special spot in the rock and roll shows for his own fiery brand of blues-soul shouting. He was so wild and enduring while performing in front of a predominately all black audience than say even a Mick Jagger and the late Jim Morrison were in front of their own respective white fans. While Jagger and Morrison would try to simulate or act out the part of a macho man, no one could come as close to being so brazingly brave while performing as Gorgeous George was. Whether the latter two saw George perform in person is not really known. This pompous spectacular black entertainer wsa the real thing and he completely fitted the role as the complete (Soul) artist.

With a minimum of security afforded to him, Gorgeous George still was actually among the very first showmen to go to such extremes as to actually risk life and limb in the name of rock and roll. The gorgeous one had at one time the most death defying act in rock. He is also the first ever to not only have his clothes literally torn off his body from top to bottom by his screaming followers, but he was the forerunner to Ozzie Osbourne, Grand Funk, Iggy Pop, David Lee Roth, Freddie Mercery and Roger Daltry to show off his bare chest on stage.

During a rock and roll show at Kansas City in October, 1961, Gorgeous George kept on stomping back and forth and prancing side by side with his eyes shut as if he was into a hypnotic state at the front center edge of the stage only to hurl himself into the frenzied

crowd of fans below who would rip and tear him apart
in trying to snitch any kind of souvenir to take home. It
didn't matter whether or not they could tear off a piece
of a T-shirt, a piece of his own scalp or even any of
his undergarments. After climbing back on stage, he
would grab a microphone and collapse onto the floor
while screaming loudly, "I've got to find me a part-time
love," acting out the part of a starving bluesman. This
incredible entertainer with a touch of bravery, brought
this hot set to an unrehearsed climax that no other performer could actually match again. For the third time in
a row, Gorgeous George started his hypnotic ritual once
again. This wild crazed ladies man with the Little
Richard PomPadour, danced, pranced, stomped and
stammered on the edge of the stage just inches away
from certain annihilation. This Atlanta native brought
about the true meaning of sex and rock when he
merged the two together into a total rush of an
orgasmic sensation. By this time, the crowd was out of
control all around the stage on the auditorium arena
floor when he raised his arms as he leaped and threw
himself away like a kamikaze pilot to the hungry young
wet lionesses below. It was mass hysteria as shirt, pants,
socks and all undergarments were savagely ripped from
his heaving flesh. The security police were rushed into
an almost unbearable emergency situation in order to
save Gorgeous George from possible death as well as
scandal. Several attendants rushed to the front left side
of the stage with a huge dark blanket while quickly
pushing the fans away in order to roll him up in it and
carried the beleaguered singer backstage to safety, only
to let him do his crazy antics all over again at another
place on down the road.

Gorgeous George was the last singer who performed
on the show that unforgettable night and not suprisingly
he stole the show away from the better known acts including the Vibrations, Ted Taylor, and Bo Diddley.

Gorgeous George was so incredible that memorable October night even to the point that in spite of the abscence of the show's two main headliners, Jackie Wilson and Jerry Lee Lewis, nobody asked for their money back.

Not only did Gorgeous George perform so daringly on these packaged rock and roll extravaganzas, he also hosted them as well. Each and every time he would step out in a different shiny bright suit with a colored tie and coat pocket handkerchief to match. When he would introduce Jeanette "Baby" Washington, this black knight in shining armour would be all dressed out in a blinding red suit only to introduce the following artists such as the Bo Diddley Trio in an all silver or blue outfit.

This forgotten talented and yet ever so colorful southerner with a robust personality and sophisticated charm to match could easily be tagged "The Burt Reynolds of the South." Gorgeous George recorded for his own hometown label, Peachtree Records in 1968 with such soul luminaries at Mitty Collier, Peg Leg Moffet, and the Dynamics. Gorgeous George also recorded with the Fab Three on the Hale (105) label with their thriller called "Teach Me."

Bunker Hill was one of the strangest and yet most compelling of all the early sixties hit makers. Bunker's giant nursery rhyme which was styled in a rhythm and blues-pop vein was "Hide and Seek Parts One and Two." Bunker Hill's antics on stage included singing his aforementioned song live on stage while bracing himself and standing completely on his head with only a small pillow providing him with any degree of support.

Soul, as well as rock had some very important singers to its fore. Soul was synonymous with rock and roll during the first generation of their popularity. Many artists crossed over back and forth from rock to soul and vica versa. Ray Charles could rock with the best of them and Jerry Lee Lewis was a tremendous soul screamer during the mid-sixties when his producers decided to move into that particular genre. His version of Bobby "Blue" Bland's "Turn on Your Love Light" was full of punch and drive. Many of the rock and soul stars even crossed over into country including Bobby Bland, Jerry Lee Lewis, Conway Twitty, Ray Charles, and dozens of others.

Soul like rock was a very viable medium in the fifties and sixties. For example, many of the top girl groups came from the soul field into rock such as the Shirelles and the Supremes featuring the lead vocals of Diana Ross. The Shirelles first clicked with "I Met Him on a Sunday" for Decca on April 12, 1958 but reached stardom with "Dedicated to the One I Love" in July, 1959. The Shirelles who featured the lead voice of Shirley Alston racked up a total of six top tenners and eleven charted tunes in the coveted top forty. Diana Ross and the Supremes had twenty-two top forty gems and seventeen tunes that placed in the top ten with twelve number one songs.

The other premier headlining rhythm and blues singers in the late fifties and early to mid-sixties achieved star status by their recordings continually crossing the soul charts into the top pop one-hundred. Solomon Burke, the Drifters, B. B. King, the Vibrations, Ruth Brown, and Bo Diddley, among others, were soon having success selling their single forty-five rpm recordings to an increasingly integrated record buying public via the top forty stations.

Sam Cooke had forty-three charted tunes on Billboard from October, 1957 to April, 1966, with such classics as "You Send Me," "Summertime," "Everybody Likes To Cha-Cha," "Cupid," "Chain Gang," "Having a Party," "Twisting the Night Away," "A Change Is Gonna' Come," "Shake," and his last chart entry, "Let's Go Steady Again."

Brook Benton, another popular headline attraction, placed forty-six songs on the playlists with five of them being top ten entries while seventeen of his recordings hitting the top forty. Benton also scored with the late balladeer, Dinah Washington in "You've Got What It Takes" and "A Rockin' Good Way" for Mercury.

Fats Domino had thirty top forty hits while a whopping sixty-six selections making the charts for him from 1956 until 1963.

Jackie Wilson placed forty-seven songs on the charts along with two other numbers he recorded with Count Basie in "For Your Precious Love," and "Chain Gang."

Jerry Butler had twenty-eight charted recordings while soulmate, Chuck Jackson racked up eighteen solid soul classics.

Bobby "Blue" Bland never made it to the top ten. The closest he got was with the soulful Latin-flavored "Call On Me" which reached up to number twenty-two before falling off the hot one-hundred in 1963.

Rock legend, Chuck Berry ironically never had a number one record either. He charted twenty-five times. The closest he ever came to the top position was in February 8, 1958, when "Sweet Little Sixteen" peaked at number two. The most popular bar song of all time and the follow-up to "Sixteen" was "Johnny B. Goode" which only got as high as number eight in April, 1958.

The twelve bar blues offerings have been researched extensively throughout the past thirty years.

Some of the top blues artists include Odetta, Elmore James, Buddy Guy, James Cotton, the real country blues (acoustical guitar accompaniment to earthy vocals) stylist — Lightnin' Hopkins, Robert Johnson, Son House, Sonny Williamson (numbers one, two and three), Blind Lemon Jefferson, Ma Rainey, Bessie Smith, Junior Wells, Roscoe Gordon, Lowell Fulsom, Otis Rush, Little Walter, and Josh White. Even rocker Chuck Berry put out some stimulating twelve bar blues ballads including "Wee Wee Hours" in the mid-fifties. Among the best modern day bluesmen are Muddy Waters, B. B. King and Bobby "Blue" Bland.

The late Muddy Waters was a legendary singer who also excelled as a guitarist and a composer. Waters started out playing Saturday night fish fries in Rolling Fork, Mississippi for fifty cents and half a bottle of moonshine.

He was born McKinley Morganfield in Rolling Fork, Mississippi in April 4, 1915. He picked up "Muddy Waters" as a childhood nickname. At thirteen, he was playing harmonica and a short time later he taught himself to play guitar.

In 1941, Muddy was recorded by Alan Lomax (who discovered Leadbelly) for the Liberty of Congress. By the late forties, Muddy migrated to Chicago and became the most popular and influential bluesman in town.

Muddy got some valuable down-home training by playing gigs with Son House and Robert Johnson.

Muddy had many hits for the Chess label out of Chicago with such down in the alley favorites in "Long Distance Call," "Hoochie Coochie Man," "Got My Mojo Workin' " and "Rollin' Stone," the latter which became the name of a British group and a magazine.

Muddy has influenced so many of today's popular artists including Mick Jagger, Chuck Berry, Eric Clapton, Johnny and Edgar Winter, Ry Cooder, and Elvin Bishop. The latter artist once related an experience he encountered in witnessing a Muddy Waters concert in Chicago while the bluesman was appearing in front of an all-black audience. "One of the best (musical) forms in dealing with people is the blues — out of the South to the North. What they (bluesmen) are concerned about is with living their life. It helps to come out of a blues background. Blues deals with real life like some guy beating the shit out of his old lady with a two by four," says Elvin candidly. "I remember seeing Muddy Waters in Chicago and he had that crowd believing him. I saw him put a Coke bottle down his trousers and chicks were waving welfare checks in front of him, just begging him to take it — for me, that's the blues. A lot of blues today is artificial fake music like the Ten Years After," he concluded.

Singer James Brown's two favorite bluesmen in Bobby "Blue" Bland and B. B. King, who collectively have a total of over sixty-five years in the music business. While appearing on a nationally televised dance show in 1975, Brown sang with and praised the blues duo of Bland and King as being the best in their trade — "They have no competition," he proclaimed.

Bobby "Blue" Bland was discovered in part by B. B. King in Memphis when King introduced Bobby to pianist, Billy "Red" Love who taught Bland how to sing the blues. King and fellow mentor, Roscoe Gordon introduced the aspiring vocalist to Samuel Bihari of Modern Records and the rest they say is history.

Bobby was once a close friend of fifties crooner, Eddie Fisher, while serving in the Army as a guest of Uncle Sam during their tenure in Korea. Bland coincidentally cut his first recording after service duty that was appropriately titled "Army Blues" for the Houston-based Duke label. After this very first recording, Bobby quickly became identifiable with his hoarse tenor moans and pleadings. These utterances have helped make Bland become a definitive trademark with modern day blues.

During an interview in 1975, Bland admittedly wanted to change direction and become more versatile by not only singing the blues in his repertoire but also start recording more country songs for his label at the time — ABC-Dunhill. "I like to sing country songs like Merle Haggard's 'Today, I Started Loving You Again,' " he admitted. Bobby simply came to the sound conclusion that "music is music."

Riley B. B. King (B. B. stands for Blues Boy) is a name that is certainly synonymous with the blues. His recordings were made and released in 1949 with Bullet Records. B. B. later moved over to the RPM label in the early fifties. B. B. King has subsequent classics on Kent and the low budget Crown Recording Company in Los Angeles in the late fifties and early sixties. King's "Sweet Sixteen" was one of the most played rhythm and blues songs on the southern r&b oriented radio stations including Dr. Jazzmo's show on XERF in Mexico during 1959-60.

Like James Brown's live Apollo Theatre 1962 LP, it was King's "Live at the Regal" for ABC Paramount in 1965 that helped define his blues legacy and this historic work helped give King a shot in the arm as far as his status as an artist is concerned.

B. B. King's appearances on all the big packaged rock and roll shows in the mid-sixties were legendary. His backup unit, the B. B. King Orchestra usually backed the other artists on the bill. One of the best tours in the late sixties occurred in the spring of 1968 when B. B. King and his musical entourage backed and supported William Bell, Barbara Acklin, Peg Leg Moffit, and Judy Clay.

This southerner who is known as the "King of the Blues" has not only achieved superstar status in his field but also has become the darling of the Hippie generation and the white blues-rock movement of the late sixties. These young war babies white bluesmen such as Michael Bloomfield, Janis Joplin, Eric Clapton, Keith Richard, Mick Jagger, the Paul Butterfield Blues Band, Bob Hite of Canned Heat have all proclaimed King to be the "Master." It is B. B. King's twelve bar modern day style that has a very distinct quality to it. This vintage bluesman picks his strings while bending and sustaining his crying-squealing notes on his guitar nicknamed "Lucille."

Unlike other bluesmen in his field, B. B. King doesn't always sing and play simultaneously. King always found that his own coordination wasn't always the best—"—trying to sing and play at the same time didn't get to me—when I'm sustaining, while I'm trying to get my breath, or think of a new line to tell you, then the guitar takes over—."

In 1972, B. B. was honored by his own peers in the recording industry by winning the Grammy Award for his brilliant upbeat blues masterpiece, "The Thrill is Gone."

He followed in white soul country-billy, Johnny Cash's footsteps by playing for prisoners behind bars. Subsequently, a live album was issued in the early seventies that was cut in Chicago appropriately called, "Live at Cook County Jail."

In the summer of 1985, King was part of the movie soundtrack to "Into the Night." As a result of the soundtrack, a video was produced that starred not only B. B. King, but his backup band on stage included some of his long time fans in Dan Aykroyd, Steve Martin and Eddie Murphy.

After thirty-seven years in the business, B. B. King is still definitely the "Master."

There were two other soul entertainers that usually never toured with any of the other r&b stars but had their own shows with each one being the only known artist on the bill. These two famous individuals—Ray Charles and James Brown were the biggest selling soul artists of the late fifties to early seventies. Both of them played instruments including the keyboards in front of sell-out arenas on the strength of their respective hits. Ray Charles alone with sixty-six charted numbers and eleven top ten favorites started with "What'd I Say" in June, 1959.

Most soul oriented artists couldn't keep up with the running tide of hits by white recording stars but Charles still scored with three number one gems with "Georgia on My Mind," (1960), "Hit the Road Jack" in 1961 and the 1962 monster classic of "I Can't Stop Loving You." These recordings were demonstrative of the crossover style perpetuated by soul genius, Ray Charles who not only recorded soul songs for Atlantic, but crossed over and cut country and western ballads for ABC-Paramount long before other crossover artists like Lionel Richie and Linda Rondstadt came along.

"Soul Brother Number One"—James Brown garnered a total of seventy chart toppers with twenty-six of them in the top forty and six top ten favorites that "Mr. Dynamite" scored with between 1965-8. His biggest evergreens during this time period were "Papa's Got a Brand New Bag," "I Got You," and the male chauvinist ballad, "It's a Man's World."

After reviewing the above, it is easy to realize that soul music has made a profound impact on popular music from the late fifties on through the sixties.

BACK TO THE FIFTIES IN THE EIGHTIES

There is a resurgence of fifties and early sixties rock and roll now in the eighties. Robert Plant, former lead vocalist of the heavy metal band, Led Zeppelin, has been going back to the roots by recording classics that were originally cut over two decades ago. Plant's Atlantic releases include Phil Phillip's 1959 hit, "Sea of Love," and Roy Brown's "Good Rockin' Tonight." George Thorogood and the Destroyers have cut Bo Diddley's "Who Do You Love," and has a hit video with the 1958 Johnny Otis original, "Willie and the Hand Jive." Ronnie Milsap in the pop-country field also has recreated the fifties doo-wopp song, "Lost in the Fifties Tonight," that has bits and pieces of the Five Satins 1956 masterpiece "In The Still of the Night," placed selectively throughout the song. Rockabilly rebels from the fifties are touring England, Belgium, Ireland, Sweden, and other points around Europe and beyond, for the fifties music fanatics and the Teddy Boys of England. Charlie Feathers, Ray Campi, Carl Perkins, Jerry Lee Lewis and many others are crossing the Atlantic to play their incredible rockin' sounds for their worldwide fans. Las Vegas is still a popular stop-over for many of the early greats of rock and roll. Jerry Lee Lewis and Ricky Nelson teamed up together for concerts in Vegas and southern California in February, 1985. Richard Nader and Tony DeLauro respectively are busy producing the various Doo Wopp shows in New York every year, while Doo-Wopp (street corner harmony) still lives with a New Jersey-based organization called "United in Group Harmony Association" who are dedicated in preserving this true fifties art form.

ZZ Topp has added the key ingredients of 1950's Texas-styled rockabilly, country and western, and blues along with amplified ear-shattering notes on their guitars and vocals to come up with their modern day version of Texas Boogie. Billy Gibbons, and the rest of the members of this popular hot Texas band, have stated through interviews with me that "Singers like George Jones are influential (on their music). We like Gene Vincent's "Be Bop-A-Lula."

Charlie Daniels has been greatly influenced by the many top country and rockabilly stars as well as jazz artists. He grew up listening and becoming influenced by the sounds of country fiddles along with the top country-billy stars like Roy Acuff, Hank Williams and Carl Perkins.

Charlie has become a superstar in the eighties by singing patriotic songs and creating country-boogie—jazz fusion type of numbers in such classics as "The South's Gonna' Do It Again" and "The Devil Went Down To Georgia."

Tanya Tucker is continuing in the tradition left by Wanda Jackson by combining successfully the basic blends of traditional country and grinding fundamental rock and roll. Her popularity remains in tact in the mid-eighties.

The Who which includes the raw untamed talents of guitarist-composer, Pete Townshend, has borrowed heavily from fifties music. Townshend's early influence was the fifties rock and roll guitarist, Link Wray, whose instrumentals such as "Rumble," "Rawhide," and "Comanche" helped set the tone for other rock guitarists for generations to come.

The Stray Cats are a band that revived and popularized rockabilly in the early eighties while the Blasters from the Los Angeles area are recreating good time rock and roll again in "I'm Shakin'," while also writing many of their own songs.

Los Lobos are a southern California Mexican band who are strong in combining the vintage rock and roll roots to their playing while also mixing some of their own Spanish-flavored heritage styles into their repertoire. The group really excells on all their own arrangements on such selections as Fats Domino's "I'm Gonna Be A Wheel Someday," and Mitch Ryder's "Devil With the Blue Dress On."

The Boss himself—Bruce Springsteen, has been deeply influenced by the rawness of the fifties music. He has been touched considerably by Elvis Presley and Gene Vincent.

His right hand man, Clarence Clemons blows a sax in the raspy fifties style that is likened to Sam "The Man" Taylor and Rusty Bryant.

Bruce's left hand man, Nils Lofgren, was a fan of many of the early rhythm and blues singers from the early sixties like Stevie Wonder and the Motown Sound.

"I love soul music—Ray Charles, Aretha Franklin, and Stevie Wonder. Besides the Beatles, I've loved old Motown with the Supremes—they had great writers. The Supremes had a lot of great songs—they (Motown) were the best, I thought," says Nils.

"My friends turned me on to it (Motown), since Jimi Hendrix is the only idol I've really ever had," he added.

Nils also feels strongly that the early format of what the classic rock and roll shows of the fifties and sixties achieved in their distinct presentations are finally coming back full circle once again—"Well, I think vaudeville is getting back into music. Even though I don't have a million dollars to spend on fancy clothes, I feel that an artist can do something himself without using a prop or something. I think it means something to the kids if the artists can do something themselves rather than just wheeling out some big prop or something. I just like your classic old show. They're (the fifties and soul artists) great entertainers. A lot of the soul shows is entertainment—and it is entertainment, and it is getting back into music today, as opposed to a lot of glitter and makeup. I'm going to expand and have a new concept called Athletic Rock, and I'm hopefully going to introduce that in a year or so. I've started it a little bit already by doing a backflip—I do have a little mini trampoline—very small about three feet in diameter and I do a little backflip at the end of the show and bang—(we're) gone off the stage. We're not football players or nothing like that but I just think it (Athletic Rock) is a good term. I think a lot of young kids today will grow up and combine sports and music, which I think that's the best two things we have in entertainment for the public."

"When I was a musician on the accordian, I really always wanted to be a professional athlete, but I wasn't big enough to do that."

"I feel I can bring sports to music—not just songs about it but I'm talking as far as attitude, you know—something that is good for both mind and body," candidly admits Lofgren.

As 1986 comes around, Nils Lofgren couldn't be any happier than he is right now in working as a guitarist and vocalist in Bruce Springsteen's "E" Street Band. Both Bruce and Nils are from New Jersey and started in music through similar circumstances by digging on fifties rock and sixties soul. They incorporated roots music with their own creative offerings and now more recently have collectively molded the right amount of ingredients into a rockin' happy sound that should keep them at the top number one position of the rock and roll ladder.

No matter how far they (the music industry) try to get away from what is the finely tuned basics of rock and roll, there is simply no escaping the roots of this popularly contemporary middle-aged art form.

EPILOGUE:
ROCK AND ROLL FOREVER

Prior to 1964, most albums that were released by the major companies like VeeJay, RCA, MGM, Colpix, and Columbia had six songs cut on each side of the disk. This was before the so-called "Concept" recordings came into being during and after 1966-67. As an unwritten rule during the pre-Beatles golden age of rock and roll, the average length of each composition was just under three minutes in duration.

The album used to be the catalyst and vehicle for the forty-five rpm disk. The record-buying public spent their hard earned dollars mainly on the single releases as opposed to buying albums. It goes without saying, that there were a lot more of a wider variety of original compositions that were marketed on the forty-five.

Kenny Gamble, one-half of the famed songwriting team of Gamble and Huff from Philadelphia, stated during an interview with the former "Tomorrow" NBC program host, Tom Snyder, stated that "The forty-five is now the vehicle for the album." Gamble felt that the public has become more sophisticated in their tastes and they have found that by buying the LP's, they get more for their money. The album releases have subsequently been packaged in a way that will help satisfy John Q. Public's appetite. Consequently, the album covers in general since 1965 have taken on a new meaning by becoming more and more a work of art. Both sex and violence have been used as vivid fantasy themes for psychedelic bands in the late sixties (e.g.—Jimi Hendrix's

"Electric Ladyland") to suicidal dimensions in punk rock and new wave stylings found in the late seventies and eighties originated in part by the Sex Pistols from England.

Earlier in 1964, the Beatles and their frequent bubble gum sounds was a gimmick that payed off for them and this funny intonation can be simply defined as the Chipmunks warbling at a slower rpm speed. "Yellow Submarine," (among others) vicariously showed that no matter what they wrote or how archaic their early songs were, the public was duped into buying their records— the common denominator was quantity over quality.

There were some exceptions whereby the Beatles could also be brilliant. Their early covers of rock classics like "Kansas City" and "Be-Bop-A-Lula" and original songs like "Yesterday" and "Something" (the latter song which was written by George Harrison is Frank Sinatra's favorite song) were able to demonstrate the unit's talented magic side.

This legendary outfit from Liverpool, England, also did in fact give credit where credit is due in mentioning their other influences. Their influences were many of rock's finest. John Lennon was the Chief Beatle who credited many of his faves as his idols in Gene Vincent, Jerry Lee Lewis, Elvis, Carl Perkins, Fats Domino, the Miracles, The Marvelettes, Earl Bostic, and Chuck Jackson.

The Beatles finally got tired of hearing themselves and after seven years of international fame, they broke away from each other. John Lennon was actually tiring from listening to Paul McCartney's syrupy and insipid songs.

In retrospect, a music critic in 1969 labeled the Beatle's music as "Chicken Rock." The Beatles actually did more to compromise rock and roll and lead it in the direction of middle of the road more than any other singular group in the history of popular music. They were talented granted, but the mop top foursome were not geniuses—they steered the record buying public away from rock not toward it. The Beatles were very original and explored new adventures. They were experimental but it was more commercial experimentation (that would sell) than it was anything else.

The Beatles rarely toured and that is a vital part of rock—just ask Jerry Lee Lewis! Getting your rocks off by performing a live show is more a satisfying orgasm than sitting alone with some goons at Graceland or sulking over some bananas at the Bahamas.

When the Dick Clark Five first debuted British Rock in America, they didn't sell out as many seats as the Beatles eventually did. During their tour of the states, the Dave Clark Five did feature Dave Clark's early style of drumming with his ta-da-da beats. Clark also came up with an idea he implemented by putting flashing red lights inside all of his drums.

Back in 1965, the Rolling Stones invaded America on the heels of the first flush of the British invasion which started in earnest in January, 1964.

The Stones were the most obnoxious of the lot in their repulsive revolutionary ideas like living together with their followers (groupies) and some of the member's satanic worship symbolism.

The Rolling Stones didn't always even sell out all of the venues in the states. For example, when they appeared at Omaha, Nebraska, the Stones didn't sell out their own concert. There was an incident when a security guard sent programs backstage for the Stones to sign and give back to him. The guard came back out with the autographed keepsakes quipping that he didn't think that any of the members of the group had taken a bath for months.

In spite of their chaotic behavior and the castration of their music, the Rolling Stones remain the embodiment of modern day rock.

Why has so much British Rock since the Beatles in 1964 been so popular for so long and why is a lot of it revolutionary in tone? One British rocker candidly explained that "With so much tradition and custom still so prevalent in my mother country, it all gets to the point when you want to bust out of that mold and try to do something different for a change!" Many English groups want to experiment and so many of them have been successful in trying out original concepts. Jethro Tull, the Beatles, Led Zeppelin, Pink Floyd, and Who and Boy George have all had one major thing in common and that is trying out untested ideas that have never really been tried out before. For example, the Beatles added different instruments to their repertoire such as the melotron, and sitar on "Norwegian Wood," while Jethro Tull electronically wired in his flute to make it sound like a singing guided missile, Led Zeppelin fostered heavy metal and the Who inspired punk. Pink Floyd as a group theatrically performed with an amplified psychedelic steel guitar equipped with specific effects like thunderous storm noises and an emission of gusts of smoke. Boy George has become more popular as the boy turned girl next door.

There used to be over three hundred record companies in the late fifties and early sixties. Today, that total number has been dwindled down to under twenty-six major companies. These few companies and MTV Video dictate the trend and direction that the crossover hybrid sounds have been caste and molded into which can be described and tagged as Corporate Rock.

Also, the process of making it in the rock and roll big time is getting too expensive for anyone to try unless there is a super rich sponsor backing up a prospective artist's career. For example, it takes nearly two-hundred thousand dollars to successfully launch an artist and a minimum of fifty thousand bucks for a video on MTV which helps control and dictates the trends. It seems as though weird and obnoxious behavior is in and being a straight person is out. The more rude and tacky an artist becomes, the better he seems to impress and sell.

The new technology of automation in society has escalated and more than doubled since January, 1964, to the point where twenty years later, the techno-revolution has been able to re-structure the entertainment industry into a contrived artificial medium. Music has gone from vocal prowess to electronic madness whereby stale synthesizers talk like people and science fiction scripts are utilized in videos whereby androids behave like androgynous heathens.

Fabian, Elvis, Bobby Rydell, Rick Nelson, Jerry Lee Lewis, Brook Benton and the other golden greats didn't have to use gimmicks to sell their natural talents. Bobby Rydell was always technically a better crooner than say a Mick Jagger while James Brown actually pioneered Jagger's swagger. Bobby Hatfield and Bill Medley even went so far as to tag Jagger as a "Clown."

Today's rock guitarists cloud their mistakes by playing at one-hundred and twenty decibals and beyond, which deafens eardrums but makes money for today's hucksters, while in pre-Beatle times, the groups and soloists had to rely on sheer natural ability along with a minimum of electronic gadgetry to mold their music into classic material.

As 1985 came to an end, there is new hope that popular music has come around full circle to a certain extent. Jazz, blues, rockabilly, and other expressive forms are picking up more steam. There are singers like Sade, the Klique, the Manhattans, Bruce Springsteen and Shakin' Stevens, who are all bringing back the roots of rock and roll. On the other hand, some of today's bigger singers that have an early sixties girl group sound is the New York-based singers like Cindy Lauper, who helps bridge yesterday and today in her musical stylings, but her image still remains as a product of punk hype.

How many people survive changing trends in rock and roll? Except for the British who always are around, very few viable artists maintain any longevity as far as chart action is concerned. Tina Turner is one that made a miraculous comeback. But, for the most part, few survive the public's fickle ever-changing tastes.

What are some of the great early rockers doing now? Many of them are in gospel music like Wayne Cockran and Dion while many others are entertaining their lifetime fans in night clubs and mini-concert dates.

There is one artist profile that is a biographical sketch similar to so many others in a midwest musician-vocalist by the name of Bugsy Maugh who was the kingpin of the rockers in the late fifties and sixties in and around the Saint Joseph, Missouri area.

Bugsy recorded for Steve Alaimo's Criteria Studios in Miami during 1960. He played on Fred Milton's Little Richard-styled rocker in "Barbie Barbie" for the Skyway label.

Bugsy later filled in for Jerry Lee Lewis at a concert date in 1959. He also later moved to Omaha in 1966 and played the electric bass behind such luminarios as Aretha Franklin, Buddy Miles, Wilson

Pickett and many others too numerous to mention. He eventually was hired by Chicago blues-rock vocalist, Paul Butterfield and recorded on the Paul Butterfield Blues Band's biggest selling Electra album, "The Resurrection of Pigboy Crabshaw" in 1967. Bugsy's roommate was Elvin Bishop and the two of them were part of different publicity stunts while Butterfield and them played some New York City dates. One of their assigned stunts was a guitar promotion for a name brand and they were required to stand in a streetside trash can for some publicity shots.

After two solo albums for Dot Paramount and some track recording sessions for the late Janis Joplin's group, the Full Tilt Boogie Band, Bugsy returned to his roots and got married in Saint Joseph. He proceeded to play in various bar bands. However, the Drunk Driving laws in the state of Missouri are now tougher with more teeth in them and this has caused a thirty percent drop in bar traffic. Consequently, the demand for live bands are at a minimum. Bugsy has now decided to quit music and go into trucking. He says that there is very little music today that inspires him. At last report though, Bugsy is working some gigs in the Minnesota region. In his talk about retiring from music, Bugsy Maugh isn't kidding anyone—rocking is still in his blood.

There are many record collectors of fifties and sixties rock and roll. These fanatics are keeping the early spirit of rock alive by organizing and attending record conventions all over the states as well as Canada, Belgium and points beyond. (See rare disk inserts.)

What has happened to some of the golden greats? There is one instance whereby Mark Dinning reports that he last heard that Jimmy ("Handy Man"—"Good Timin'") Jones washes dishes within the confines of the man made stone caverns of New York City.

Beach music has been what some rock and rhythm and blues enthusiasts have tagged their favorite timeless classics. In the Carolinas, these rock and roll buffs have resurrected such an oldie but goodies as Maurice Williams ("Stay") and he has been tagged the "King of Beach Music." Beach Music is essentially what rock and roll was all about in the first place—it is good-time dance music. Whether it be a Chuck Jackson evergreen like "Any Day Now" or a Hank Ballard and the Midnighter's mover in "Finger Poppin' Time," the venues that feature Beach Music are booking these very artists who sang the aforementioned originals (among others) once again. The old adage is still true—you can't keep a good thing down or away for very long. Other promoters and night club owners around the country are starting to realize where the basics of rock and roll originality came from, and now want to book these pioneering originator's because the marketplace for merchandising and packaging fifties and sixties recording artists are in demand, along with vintage videos of actual rock and roll movies and concerts from over twenty years ago. Bruce Springsteen always knew where it all came from—Elvis, his biggest influence, and fellow blue collar rebel who sang to and for the people also in Gene Vincent. Other classic singers like the Clovers and Bobby Day are playing the Beach Music and chitlin circuits in the 1980's while the news media gives these top rated acts little or no attention—preferring to cover instead the latest crude being imported to the states from Great Britain or even giving space to American bands that try and sound like the Beatles in REO Speedwagon.

In spite of all the negatives and positives that are both readily found in the history of rock and roll music, there is one sure-fire truism—as long as the heart beats, there will always be rock and roll.

Above Ray Charles, Chuck Jackson with the late Clarence Quick (Del Vikings) and Jerry Lee Lewis' 1958 backup band Volcanos